INHERITING THE KINGDOM

INHERITING THE KINGDOM

HEAVENLY LIVING FOR EARTH-BOUND SAINTS

Matt 25: 34 *Then shall the King say unto them on his right hand, Come, ye blessed of my Father, inherit the kingdom prepared for you from the foundation of the world:*

Gordon Lang

Copyright © 2009 by Gordon Lang.

Library of Congress Control Number: 2009906842
ISBN: Hardcover   978-1-4415-5383-6
               Softcover   978-1-4415-5382-9

All rights reserved. No part of this book may be reproduced or transmitted in any form or by any means, electronic or mechanical, including photocopying, recording, or by any information storage and retrieval system, without permission in writing from the copyright owner.

This book was printed in the United States of America.

To order additional copies of this book, contact:
Xlibris Corporation
1-888-795-4274
www.Xlibris.com
Orders@Xlibris.com

CONTENTS

INTRODUCTION 7
    Matt. 25:34

PLANTING MUSTARD 9
    Matt. 13:31

BAKING BREAD 15
    Matt. 13:33

DISCOVERING HIDDEN TREASURE 19
    Matt 13:34

WEEDING THE FIELD 24
    Matt 13:38

SHOPPING FOR THE BEST 28
    Matt 13:35

SEPARATING THE CATCH. 33
    Matt. 13:47

RECONCILING ACCOUNTS 37
    Matt 18:23

ANTICIPATING PAYDAY 43
    Matt 20:1

SETTING THE TABLE. 49
    Matt 22:2

EXPECTING THE GROOM. 55
    Matt 25:1

ASSESSING THE RISK 60
    Matt. 25:14

FEEDING THE HUNGRY 65
    Matt 25:34 & 35

SATISFYING THE THIRSTY 69
    Matt 25:34 & 35

ENTERTAINING STRANGERS 72
    Matt 25:34 & 35

CLOTHING THE NAKED 75
    Matt 25:34 & 35

VISITING THE SICK 79
    Matt 25:34 & 35

MINISTERING IN PRISON 83
    Matt 25:34 & 35

LESSONS FROM THE PLAYGROUND 88
    Matt 18:3

BAGGAGE HANDLERS ANONYMOUS 92
    Matt: 19:24

FIRST THINGS FIRST 97
    Matt 6:33

THE KINGDOM WITHIN 101
    Luke 17:21

INHERITING THE KINGDOM

INHERITING THE KINGDOM

HEAVENLY LIVING FOR EARTH-BOUND SAINTS

Matt 25: 34 *Then shall the King say unto them on his right hand, Come, ye blessed of my Father, inherit the kingdom prepared for you from the foundation of the world:*

Gordon Lang

Copyright © 2009 by Gordon Lang.

Library of Congress Control Number: 2009906842
ISBN: Hardcover   978-1-4415-5383-6
             Softcover   978-1-4415-5382-9

All rights reserved. No part of this book may be reproduced or transmitted in any form or by any means, electronic or mechanical, including photocopying, recording, or by any information storage and retrieval system, without permission in writing from the copyright owner.

This book was printed in the United States of America.

To order additional copies of this book, contact:
Xlibris Corporation
1-888-795-4274
www.Xlibris.com
Orders@Xlibris.com

CONTENTS

INTRODUCTION 7
    Matt. 25:34

PLANTING MUSTARD 9
    Matt. 13:31

BAKING BREAD 15
    Matt. 13:33

DISCOVERING HIDDEN TREASURE 19
    Matt 13:34

WEEDING THE FIELD 24
    Matt 13:38

SHOPPING FOR THE BEST 28
    Matt 13:35

SEPARATING THE CATCH 33
    Matt. 13:47

RECONCILING ACCOUNTS 37
    Matt 18:23

ANTICIPATING PAYDAY 43
    Matt 20:1

SETTING THE TABLE 49
    Matt 22:2

EXPECTING THE GROOM 55
    Matt 25:1

ASSESSING THE RISK 60
    Matt. 25:14

FEEDING THE HUNGRY 65
    Matt 25:34 & 35

SATISFYING THE THIRSTY 69
   Matt 25:34 & 35
ENTERTAINING STRANGERS 72
   Matt 25:34 & 35
CLOTHING THE NAKED 75
   Matt 25:34 & 35
VISITING THE SICK 79
   Matt 25:34 & 35
MINISTERING IN PRISON 83
   Matt 25:34 & 35
LESSONS FROM THE PLAYGROUND 88
   Matt 18:3
BAGGAGE HANDLERS ANONYMOUS 92
   Matt: 19:24
FIRST THINGS FIRST 97
   Matt 6:33
THE KINGDOM WITHIN 101
   Luke 17:21

INTRODUCTION

Then shall the King say unto them on his right hand, Come, ye blessed of my Father, inherit the kingdom prepared for you from the foundation of the world:
                                                                Matt. 25:34

Inheritance, it's a concept that goes back as far as Adam, but is just as relevant today. It can be the source of the most bountiful of blessings, or the cause of the most bitter disputes. Since the dawn of civilization, the questions surrounding the rights of inheritance have possibly raised more controversy that any other subject in our society. What happens to someone's personal wealth when that person departs from this temporal life? How will his acquired wealth be distributed, and who is entitled to benefit from that distribution? In anticipation of such an event, it is prudent to make arrangements—a process which, in legal terms, we call "making a last will and testament". In Old Testament times the legal process was known as the principle of birthright, and was restricted to the oldest son. With the passage of time, however, the laws were extended to include any or all members of the family unit. Within the last century, the legal definition has been further revised to include any acquaintance of the testator at his or her discretion.

Any discussion regarding inheritance involves at least two distinct persons. First, there must be the testator—the one who is preparing for his demise. In an act of foresight, this person makes certain decisions regarding the disposition of his wealth upon the eventuality of his death. Additionally, we must include, in such a discussion, the heir(s)—the one(s) who will be the recipients of the wealth of the testator after his death.

In order to effect the laws regarding inheritance, it becomes evident that certain prerequisites must be met. First of all, as the writer of Hebrews points out, *there must, of necessity, be the death of the testator*. Prior to the death of the testator, the testament, or document has no effect. But, after the death of the testator, his written *will* becomes the law by which provision is made for his family, and his estate is distributed. Additionally, there must be some type of relationship between the testator and the heir. This could be a blood relationship, a close friendship, or even a more corporate relationship—for example, members of a social group to which the testator belonged. In a spiritual application of these principles, it becomes apparent that all believers have been given a part in the greatest legacy of all time.

Since it is the Kingdom of Heaven that is the subject of our discussion, it becomes evident that it is the will or testament of Almighty God that sets in motion the process of *inheriting the kingdom*. The apostle Peter states that God's will is that all mankind should come to a place of repentance for their sins, and consequently that none should perish. At the same time, Paul says that *the unrighteous shall not inherit the kingdom of heaven*. We may conclude, then, that at the end of time as we know it, there will be two groups of eternal souls of mankind. The first group will be the heirs of the kingdom—those who will hear the commendation of the Father when He says—*Well done, good and faithful servants. Enter into the joy of your Lord*. The second group will consist of those who did not do the will of the Father during their earthly lifetime, and, consequently, are to be *cast into the outer darkness*. Certainly, with very little debate, the majority of mankind would rather be a part of the former group—but how does one become a member of that group? And how can we be sure that our membership is current at any particular point in time?

This book seeks to provide answers to these questions by drawing principles from the various analogies that Jesus presented during His earthly teachings. Undoubtedly, every heir of the kingdom will be able to see a mirror image of himself somewhere in these real-life scenarios. In so doing, we will discover eternal principles which we may use as guidelines for conduct as we engage in the process of Inheriting the Kingdom which has been prepared for us since before the foundation of the world.

PLANTING MUSTARD

He presented another parable to them, saying, "The kingdom of heaven is like a mustard seed, which a man took and sowed in his field;

Matt. 13:31

Living next door to the Harbingers was NOT easy! If it wasn't one thing, it was something else. Danny's mind went back to the scene that had occurred last month when six-year old James had scurried into their neighbor's yard in pursuit of his soccer ball. In the manner of children, James took little notice of the meticulous flower garden that adorned the side of the house—his only thought was to retrieve the wandering ball. That evening, just as the news program was concluding, Danny had answered the telephone only to be greeted with a tirade of *how irresponsible his children were*, and that *he should be teaching them to have a little more respect for other people's property*!

Then there was the fiasco about the fence. In response to the complaint regarding the errant soccer ball, Danny had decided to build a fence between the two properties. A hesitant call to the Harbingers regarding their concurrence to such an undertaking was met with the dour expression of—"well something had better be done to keep those brats out of our yard!" It wasn't until the fence project was nearing completion, that he received a curt telephone call from George Harbinger informing him that the fence was six inches over the property line—and what was he going to do about it?! What *could* he do about it? After a number of calls to city hall, and a $300.00 bill for the survey, it was determined that the fence was indeed within the limits of his own property. As for the costs of the survey, George had reluctantly agreed to pay for half—but Danny hadn't seen any cheque yet.

His reverie was broken by the sound of the Harbingers Doberman hound once again snarling and barking, straining at his leash, trying to intimidate some passing cyclist. Long after the presumed danger had passed, the dog was still complaining vehemently. It wasn't so bad during the day, but when the dog decided that the wind blowing against the shed door at 2:00 AM was definitely an intruder, that was absolutely aggravating. It didn't seem to matter that the dog was being a nuisance to others, Danny was informed that he was 'simply doing his job'. The children were terrified to pass too close to the fence, and the mailman had complained about the animal's aggressiveness, but still, the Harbingers claimed it was their right to keep the dog for the purposes of protecting their property.

"Earth to Danny.!" the melodic voice of his wife, Sarah, abruptly drew Danny back to the present. He turned to acknowledge her presence—her face was a picture of concern. Had James gotten into trouble with the neighbors again? "Did you know that Doreen Harbinger was taken to the hospital early this morning? She was complaining of chest pains again. I hope nothing is wrong with the baby." Sarah's voice reflected an element of apprehension. Danny had forgotten that the Harbingers were even expecting an addition to their family. He shuddered to think about how the couple would cope with a 'worst-case scenario'. Suddenly, George's confrontational attitude was of little concern in the light of the dreadful possibilities.

The light was on at the Harbinger's that night when Danny parked the car in the driveway. The look on Sarah's face, as he shut the door behind him, confirmed his worst suspicions. "They lost the baby this morning!" Sarah mumbled—it was plain to see that she had been weeping over the plight of their neighbors. Danny winced in emotional pain as he remembered their own struggle when Sarah had miscarried two years before James' birth. At least they had a spiritual family then, from which they could draw strength in their time of grief—the Harbingers would not have such a luxury. As they stood in each other's embrace, fighting their rising emotions, Danny mumbled a prayer that God would comfort George and Doreen in their sorrow, and that somehow the situation could be used for His glory.

"I took the last of that casserole over to George so that he wouldn't have to worry about cooking supper for himself. He said that Doreen would be in the hospital for the rest of the week. Oh Danny, he looked so alone and confused. I tried to tell him that we understood his feelings, but

I don't know if he believed me." Sarah's eyes were brimming with tears now, and Danny shared her emotion as he wondered how to reach out to George with the love of Christ. He recalled their own disappointment and Sarah's sense of personal failure at the loss of her pregnancy, and wondered how the Harbingers would survive the impending emotional storm.

The doorbell rang at 10:30 Saturday morning, just as Danny was making the final preparations for teaching tomorrow's Adult Bible class. Slightly perturbed by the interruption, he opened the door to face a harried looking George Harbinger. "I am sorry to bother you, Danny", his embarrassment was evident in his tone of voice. "I'm supposed to pick up Doreen at the hospital in half an hour, but my car won't start. I must have left the park lights on when I put it away last night. Could I impose on you to give me a boost?"

"No problem, George," Danny replied, "I'll get my cables from the garage and be right over." As he headed for the back door, he winked at Sarah who had been listening to the conversation from the kitchen.

"Would it be easier just to take our van to the hospital?" Sarah suggested, "it would be much more comfortable for Doreen I'm sure."

"I'm sure glad I've got you!" Danny exulted in his practical wife as he kissed her good-bye. "We should be back by 1:00."

George already had the hood of his car open when Danny pulled the van in front of it. "Hop in," Danny invited as he held the door open.

"But I thought . . ." George stammered.

"She'll be much more comfortable in the van," Danny reiterated Sarah's suggestion, "and beside that, I'm pretty well free for the rest of the day anyway."

"You really don't need to do that," George began to protest, but seeing the resolve in Danny's face, he reluctantly positioned himself in the driver's seat and fastened the seatbelt. "Why are you guys doing this?" George stammered, "Sarah with the casserole last night, now you with the van today?" The wonder in his voice conveyed the fact that the situation was totally incomprehensible to him.

"Because we're neighbours" the words were out of Danny's mouth before he gave them much thought. It was a perfectly logical explanation in *his* mind.

"But I've been so . . ." George groped for the correct word.

"Grumpy??" Danny tried to supply the ending to the sentence. "Listen, George," he continued, "when Sarah told you last night that we know what you are going through, it wasn't just an expression." He proceeded to share their testimony of trial by the same fire, and how the Lord had been their strength when they needed Him so desperately. George listened with rapt attention, surprised at the similarity of their experiences, but profoundly moved by the difference in the manner of resolution for the two families.

"I would never have known", George stammered, "you seem so 'normal'"—it was the only word that came to his mind. "And you say James was born a few years later? That's what scares Doreen the most—she's afraid we won't ever be able to have another child." His voice quivered slightly as he expressed the last thought. "I'd better be on my way," he forced himself back to the harsh reality of his present situation. "And thanks again for the use of the van."

"Take care, George", Danny admonished, securely closing the van door. "And George—we're praying for you!", Danny almost surprised himself with the afterthought.

"Yeah, thanks, we'll need that!" George conceded as he turned to back the van from the driveway.

"God, be with them, comfort them, and draw them to Yourself", Sarah breathed the prayer as she stood beside Danny, watching the receding tail lights until the van turned the corner.

"I should go over and see how Doreen is doing", Sarah mused. It was Monday morning and they hadn't seen any sign of life next door at all yesterday, but then, they hadn't been home much with their normal Sunday activities. When George had returned the van on Saturday, he had advised them that the hospital had sent Sarah home with the directive to get plenty of rest. As she rang the doorbell it occurred to her that Doreen may not be up to answering the door yet. A pallid-looking Doreen hesitantly opened the door, and Sarah was immediately sorry for having disturbed her.

"I'm sorry to have bothered you," Sarah stammered awkwardly, "I just wanted to check and see how you are doing."

Doreen offered an embarrassed smile. "I'm getting better," she tried to sound normal, "but the doctor said I'll need plenty of bed rest for another two weeks at least. We wanted to thank-you again for the use of your van, I don't know what we would have done without it." The look on her face registered emotional weariness and heart-felt pain.

"Can I make you some tea?" Sarah offered, remembering how soothing it felt during her time of grief. Not waiting for an answer, she made her way to the kitchen and began to search for the ingredients.

"Excuse the mess," Doreen called from the living room, "I just haven't felt up to cleaning the past few days." The sink was almost full of dirty dishes, and the stove was spotted with left-over supper.

"Not a problem," Sarah tried to soothe her, "I know the feeling." Without another word, she turned the hot water tap to 'on', and began to arrange the dishes in the sink for washing. Within ten minutes the sink was empty, and the clean dishes were once again in the cupboard. Doreen sat, reclining on the couch with a cup of hot tea in her hand.

"I still don't understand all of this," Doreen began, not quite knowing how to broach the subject. "I feel like such a failure—like I've given George the ultimate 'let-down'. He was so excited when I told him that we were going to be parents." For the next few minutes the feelings that she had been so successfully hiding began to tumble from her mouth without any prompting from Sarah.

"Oh Lord, give me the words . . ." Sarah prayed silently. Then she began to share her own story with Doreen. She explained her feelings, her fears, and Danny's reaction, as Doreen listened with rapt attention. Every point she made, Doreen could identify with, until she came to the part about how the church family had given her so much support.

"That's what I need right now," Doreen admitted, "I feel like I'm carrying this all by myself. I know that George is disappointed—I don't know if it's more the situation or me that he's upset with." Sarah's eyes brimmed with tears as she recalled struggling with the same questions. Over the next few days, Danny and Sarah took every opportunity to maintain contact with George and Doreen. Whether it was a friendly "Hi Neighbor!" over the fence, or a simple telephone call to say "how are you doing today?", slowly the walls began to crumble.

It was Saturday morning once more. The telephone rang as Danny was putting the final touches on his Sunday School lesson for tomorrow. As he picked up the receiver, the voice of George Harbinger didn't wait for any salutations. "What time does church start tomorrow morning?" he asked determinedly. Danny almost fell over the end of the couch in his excitement. After explaining the normal Sunday schedule, he agreed to meet George and Doreen at the church in time for Sunday School. *The kingdom of heaven is like a mustard seed, which a man took and sowed in his field . . .*—the text of tomorrow's lesson took on an especially relevant meaning, as Danny closed his eyes and prayed for God's wisdom in sharing that lesson with his adult students.

Mustard seed, Jesus explained, is the smallest of all seeds, but when it is mature, it is like a tree to which the birds come and nest in its branches. It is interesting that in another context, Jesus used the mustard seed to illustrate the amount of faith needed to move the mountains of circumstance in our lives. In order to advance the Kingdom of Heaven among men, we need not look to the quantity or volume of our faith. We simply need to understand that, as we are faithful in planting the Word of God, He will give the increase. Whether it is by direct discourse, or, more subtly, by our acts of love, our ultimate duty is to plant the seeds. Many times, when a situation presents itself, we tend to think—*what difference will our actions make?* The opportunity may seem insignificant at the time, but in the perspective of eternity, it has the potential to make a world of difference. As we are obedient to the instructions of the Holy Spirit, we will be able to look at our lives in retrospect, and see that God has caused the seemingly insignificant seeds that we sowed to grow into a mature plant within His kingdom.

We might consider that there was another reason that Jesus used the illustration of mustard seed in regard to the kingdom of Heaven. When we think of mustard, what comes to mind? For many of us, the word would bring memories of the common culinary condiment used to enhance the flavor of certain meats. In such an illustration, we see another application for Jesus teaching. It would be encouraging for many of us to realize that the Kingdom of Heaven produces a certain flavor within believers that makes them more palatable, whether it be to other members of the Body or to non-believers. The desire for the sincere meat of the Word is a commendable trait for any maturing believer, but the meat often becomes so much more attractive to the hungry diner when it is enhanced by an adequate portion of spiritual mustard.

BAKING BREAD

He spoke another parable to them, "The kingdom of heaven is like leaven, which a woman took and hid in three pecks of flour until it was all leavened."

Matt. 13:33

It was tax season once again, and the office was humming with the excitement of trying to get everything done. The client list was building every day in response to the recent advertisements in the local newspaper, as well as the radio-advertising program that Brian Parks had sold him. George looked dismally at the rising pile of forms that filled his in-basket and knew that he would never make it to the meeting tonight. Reluctantly, he picked up the receiver and dialed his home number. After the third ring, the melodic voice of his wife, Doreen, greeted him with a vibrant "Hello George—yes, supper's just about ready. I'm just waiting for the roast to brown a little more!"

"Ah, the advantages of 'call-display'", George thought as he began to relate to Doreen the pressures of the work that was threatening to hide every square inch of his desktop. "Doreen, Darling, I just wanted to let you know . . ."

" . . . That you won't make it home in time for the meeting tonight!" Doreen completed the sentence for him. "George, this is the third week that we have had to excuse ourselves. Are you sure that your work can't wait for three hours tonight?" It annoyed him slightly that she didn't understand the importance of pleasing his clients, but her point about their increased absence from the mid-week functions at church was certainly valid. They talked at length about the situation, and, as they talked, the suggestions that Doreen made began to convict George with an increasing fervor. In fact, it began to make perfect sense in his mind that by shuffling some of his workload, maybe putting in a few extra hours tomorrow evening, he could, indeed, take Doreen to tonight's meeting. *"Seek ye first the kingdom of God and His righteousness . . ."* she quoted the text of Pastor Mark's sermon from last Sunday. But George was already convinced.

"You say that supper is almost ready?" George asked, and received confirmation. "I'll be home within half an hour—we should still have time to make the meeting". As he hurriedly cleared his desk in preparation for tomorrow's work, George was struck with the thought of how different this was from last year's tax season. Twelve months ago, he probably would have worked until nine o'clock or later, just because there was 'work to do', without even thinking to call home to explain. Now, because of the admonition of his sweet wife, he was postponing some work for tomorrow in search of the fulfillment of their hunger for the word of God.

"Darling Doreen . . ." he mused, as he walked to the parkade to retrieve his car. Yes, a lot had happened in the last twelve months. One short year ago, he certainly would not have referred to her in such endearing terms, and he definitely would not have allowed her to speak a word of correction to him. But, since Pastor Mark had invited them to that 'Couples Retreat' at Banner's Cove Resort last September, he had begun to view her in a totally different light. Rather than competing with her for pre-eminence in the affairs of the family, he now understood that she was a 'fellow-heir' in the Kingdom of Heaven. Yes, things certainly had changed in their marriage relationship—for the better! George made a mental note to thank Doreen later for her fortitude and her wise counsel regarding their spiritual priorities.

He heard the screaming of the sirens, and instantly checked his speedometer. No, he wasn't exceeding the speed limit. Glancing in the rear-view mirror, he saw the flashing red lights of an approaching ambulance. Pulling to a stop at the curbside, he once again felt the rising panic that now accompanied the presence of any emergency vehicle. Since Doreen had suffered a miscarriage of their first pregnancy last year, George had an indescribable feeling of empathy for anyone in a crisis situation. *"Oh God"*, he prayed, as he pulled back onto the deserted street, *"would You be Lord of that situation . . ."* Once again, the wonder of the changes in his life and in his emotions impressed him. Last year, he would simply have been annoyed at the inconvenience of having to give the right-of-way to the emergency vehicle, without considering the personal drama that was taking place. *"Keep that person, whoever they might be, in the hollow of Your hand . . ."* he continued to pray as the flashing lights and the wailing siren receded in the distance.

"Well, we made it!" George whispered to Doreen as they took their place in the sanctuary, just as Pastor Mark was about to start the Bible study. Everyone bowed for the opening prayer as they invited the Holy Spirit to illumine their minds to the Word of God.

"The kingdom of heaven is like leaven, which a woman took and hid in three pecks of flour until it was all leavened." Pastor Mark read the text for the evening's Bible Study. As the evening progressed, the group discussed how, in each of their experiences, the principles of the kingdom had slowly, but surely, invaded every area of their lives.

"Three pecks of flour . . ." George mused, as he considered how the Kingdom of Heaven had effected his relationship to his personal family, his church family, and even total strangers . . .

Often, when Jesus referred to leaven, it was in relation to the effect of sin in the believer's life. Certainly, we can all relate to the allegory of how the presence of sin soon begins to spread and take control of ever-increasing portions of our lives. But in this instance, Jesus used the same figure of speech to describe the effect of the kingdom of Heaven in the life of the yielded believer. It may begin with a very small portion of our lives, but *as we grow in grace, and in the knowledge of our Lord and Saviour—Jesus Christ*, we find that His love and grace begins to spread to other parts of our being. Before long, we notice ourselves considering all of our thoughts, words, and deeds, in the light of the Scriptures. Much like the phenomenal growth of the mustard seed, the leaven starts as a very small amount, but rather than becoming a visible plant, it's advancement is much more subtle. In fact, at times, one may wonder if anything is really 'happening', but as we continue to believe in faith, slowly but surely, we realize that changes are beginning to take place.

The woman in Jesus' illustration knew the effect that the leaven would have on the flour into which it was added. In terms of today's economy, the amount that Jesus indicated would compute to approximately nine gallons, or, more currently, 42 litres. The volume seems to be a bit excessive, but, judging from other uses of the term, it would appear that the amount corresponds to a common 'baking' of that day. Certainly, it was a large volume of dough. Still, slowly, but surely, the leavening agent began to effect the entire baking, and the process did not come to an end until 'the whole amount was leavened'.

As we enter the kingdom, it may seem to be a formidable task to anticipate yielding every part of our being to the control of the Holy Spirit. Still, as we are faithful to our calling in Christ, we will often be pleasantly surprised at the steady advance of the effects of the kingdom in our lives. Such an experience should be the ultimate goal of every believer until we realize that, as the Apostle Paul states, *in Him we live, and move, and have our being.*

DISCOVERING HIDDEN TREASURE

> *"The kingdom of heaven is like a treasure hidden in the field, which a man found and hid {again;} and from joy over it he goes and sells all that he has and buys that field . . . ."*
>
> Matt 13:34

The morning sunlight was streaming through the window when Bob Graham opened one eye. With the slow dawning of consciousness came the dull ache of loneliness again. As he turned to look at the eight-by-ten photograph on the dresser, a sharp stab of pain exploded in his head. His eyes lingered on the smiling face in the picture. It had been a late night again last night, trying to find relief from the pain that plagued his body and soul. He found himself gazing once more at the empty pillow beside him, and another wave of emotion washed over him. "Sheila," he heard himself mutter, "whatever happened to us?" Like a horror movie, his mind replayed the tragic chain of events over the last six months.

It started with the day he looked up from his desk to see the uniformed police officer standing in the doorway—instantly his heart dropped in fear. "Mr. Graham," he could still hear the sympathy in the officer's voice, "it's about your son Bobby . . ." Cruelly, his mind replayed the events of the following days. As if the horror of making the arrangements for the funeral, and the agony of those first few days were not enough, in the days that followed, each of them attempted to deal with their personal grief. Both had withdrawn into their separate emotional worlds, trying to handle the sorrow on their own behalf. Watching their struggles, his sister Kathy had made some pointed suggestions about seeking the counsel of her pastor, but Bob had never sought 'religious counsel' before, and he hurt too much to start now. Besides, if God were such a loving God, why would he have allowed this to take place? What was their great sin that all of this had happened to them?

Soon, the frustration of all of the unanswered questions had turned to open hostility toward each other. It wasn't long before the household had become like two armed camps. So it was not surprising to Bob, last Thursday, when Sheila had told him that she had arranged to spend some time with her mother so that she could *'sort things out'*. At least this wasn't a permanent separation, but the loneliness of an empty house still haunted him. What if she never came back? It was a question that had kept him awake for a good part of last night.

The ringing telephone broke rudely into his thoughts. He wasn't sure that he wanted to talk to anyone right now, so he let it ring. After the fifth ring, the answering machine cut in. Impatiently, he listened to the recorded preamble, then, 'after the beep' Kathy's melodic voice came over the small speaker. "Hello Bob, I know you're there," she said confidently, "and I know that you hurt too much to talk right now. I just wanted to let you know that I'm thinking of you, and I'm still praying for both of you. I love you lots, so give me a call when you feel up to it—OK? Bless you—bye." Why did she always have to say that—"bless you"? He certainly didn't feel 'blessed'! Reluctantly, he picked up the receiver, hit the speed-dial button '02' and waited for Kathy to answer.

"Bless you too!" he said, with just a hint of sarcasm in his voice, before she had a chance to say 'Hello'. Instantly he felt a stab of remorse—after-all, she was only trying to cheer him up. Kathy didn't even give a hint of taking any offense, instead, she got right into 'how was he doing?', and 'would he like to come for supper on Friday night'? Knowing how transparent he was to her, he readily accepted the invitation, just to avoid another lonely evening feasting on chicken steaks and microwave-heated corn. One statement led to another, and, before he knew it, he was confessing his hurt and loneliness to Kathy once again. He had to admit that, as much as it made him feel uncomfortably vulnerable, there was a definite sense of relief in unburdening his feelings to her.

Friday night came and went without any unusual incidents. Supper was delicious, and the conversation was stimulating. Bob listened patiently as Kathy once again proposed the idea that a 'real-life relationship' with an 'all-knowing God' would, at the very least, make his trials more bearable. His sister had never been one to simply 'follow the crowd', Bob reasoned, and the more he listened to her, the more he began to sense a growing hunger for the peace and tranquility the exuded from her. The most convincing aspect of their exchange that night was the fact that Kathy didn't condemn Bob or Sheila for the way that

Bobby's death had affected their relationship. On the contrary, honest emotions gave way to healing tears as Kathy assured him that, in God's eyes, nothing is ever beyond hope. By the time he made his way home that night, Bob found himself truly wondering if there was possibly an element of truth to Kathy's arguments. Vaguely he remembered agreeing to attend a 'grief-management' seminar that was to be held at her church the following weekend. Kathy would also attend so that she could learn how to *'minister to others'*—whatever that meant. Still, he knew that he would be grateful for her company, aware that he would definitely feel out of place with the general church-going crowd.

Wednesday evening, Sheila called again to see how he was 'holding-up'. It encouraged him to know that she was still concerned about him. In the course of the conversation, Bob mentioned the seminar that he was planning to attend with Kathy. It was clear that Sheila didn't quite know how much credibility to lend to the notion, but she certainly was not going to be openly critical. She wished him well before offering a slightly more-than-cordial 'Good-night'. "God," he prayed hesitantly, "please let this work". Then he drifted off to sleep.

It was Friday night, again, and Bob's mind was going in a hundred different directions—again. He lay in his bed, wide-awake, reviewing the principles he had heard tonight. "Grief management", the pastor had said, "is not something that you can handle on your own—you are going to need help." That was a fact that Bob had known all along, but where was he to go for help? "Remember," the words echoed in his mind, "whatever your situation may be—it is not necessarily your *fault*." Yes, that was one thing that had plagued his mind countless times—could he have done something to prevent Bobby's death? Could Sheila have done anything? Now, the whole idea of finding a scapegoat on which to lay the "blame" sounded so pitiful, and it was so very liberating to realize that he didn't have to bear the guilt anymore. Then, using the illustration of Jesus at the tomb of his friend Lazarus, the pastor had said, "Don't ever be ashamed of expressing your emotions." How many times had he stifled his rising emotions just because he had been taught that *"big boys don't cry"*?

Uncharacteristically, Bob felt an overwhelming flood of raw feelings rising within him. He panicked at the thought of an overt emotional display, but he couldn't hold it back any longer. Scenes of his son's birth, Bobby's first toddling steps, his joyful giggles, spilled over Bob's face. The loneliness of retreating to his own 'world', and the remorse of excluding Sheila from his life also rose to the surface, and was lost in mournful groanings—too deep for words. "God!", his spirit cried, "I need help"! Instinctively, he reached for the phone, and once again hit '02' on the speed dial.

When he heard Kathy's bubbly "Hello, Bob . . ." he was unable to speak. "Bob?" she repeated, as he gasped for breath between sobs, "Bob, hang in there," she encouraged, "I'll be right over!" He heard himself numbly mumble a 'thanks', then the line went dead as he hung up the phone. Waves of emotion washed over him, while he waited for Kathy to ring the doorbell. When he finally heard the chimes, he was almost too weak to even answer the door. "Oh Bob," Kathy wailed, "I am so sorry!" She wrapped her arms around him—not saying anything for several minutes as they both gave vent to their emotions. There was no condemnation, there was no sermon, she just wept with him, speaking words of comfort and encouragement as she had when they were children. Gently, she guided him to the couch and motioned for him to sit, leaving momentarily to 'put the coffee on'.

Kathy returned with a steaming cup of coffee, and continued to listen patiently as Bob emptied his soul to her. Then she reached for her Bible and began to read. *"Surely He has borne all our griefs, and carried all our sorrows . . ."* He had never heard such beautiful words, as Kathy went on to explain that Father God knew exactly how he was feeling because He had also lost His only Son. It was a totally profound concept, but, somehow, it made perfect sense. An hour passed as Kathy continued to show him just how much God loved him and cared about his situation. It didn't take any more convincing, and seemed a perfectly natural thing to do when Kathy finally asked him if he would like to 'ask Jesus to take control of his life'.

Over the next few days, Bob was impressed with the unsatiable thirst that he had to read the bible that Kathy had given him. When he talked to Sheila, even she noticed the change in his voice, and in his outlook on life. How he wanted to comfort her, to understand her feelings, to apologize for emotionally deserting her. Understandably, she was skeptical at first, but as the days turned into weeks, she also began to hope for a repairing of their relationship. It seemed that Bob was at church now every time it was open, and Sheila almost dared to believe that this change for the better was going to be permanent. It appeared quite logical then, when Bob suggested that they make an appointment to talk to the pastor about their relationship, and she accepted the opportunity without hesitation.

They sat together on the couch in the pastor's office like two school children hungrily taking in Biblical principles and instruction for building a healthy marriage. Session after session brought more changes to their relationship—definitely for the better—and Sheila became the first fruits of Bob's evangelical efforts. In fact, Bob became so excited about his newfound relationship with God, and with his wife, that it wasn't long before other family members and friends listened with undivided attention to their story.

It was Sunday night. Bob and Sheila had once again enjoyed a lively time of fellowship with the Body of Christ. As was their custom now, Bob reached for his bible to read a chapter to Sheila as she drifted off to sleep. *Again, the kingdom of heaven*, he read, *is like a treasure hid in a field, which when a man has found, he hides, and for joy over it goes and sells all that he has, and buys that field....* As he listened to Sheila's breathing become regulated in the manner of slumber, he turned out the light and pondered the treasure that he had found in this new relationship, not only with God, but also with his wife. His last thought, before he drifted off to sleep, was what it meant in his life to be totally 'sold-out' to God, and to have 'bought the field' where he had found his eternal treasure.

Many people stumble upon the kingdom of heaven totally by accident. Whether it is the result of a life-changing crisis or the consequence of a randomly spoken word by a faithful believer, the inherent value becomes unmistakably obvious. The discovery leads to an 'unspeakable joy' as the apostle Paul describes it, and a burning desire to acquire it at any cost. The man in Jesus' parable was willing to sell everything he owned in order to obtain title to the field in which his newly discovered treasure lay. Knowing that the title to the land included the rights to all that it contained, the purchaser was satisfied with the wisdom of his investment. So it is in the lives of those who, in the course of their earthly wanderings, stumble upon the treasure of the kingdom of heaven. The result must be a total surrender of all that was previously deemed to be valuable in the life of the discoverer, in order to obtain the invaluable riches that are available in Christ Jesus.

WEEDING THE FIELD

> *... the field is the world; and the good seed, these are the sons of the kingdom; and the tares are the sons of the evil ...*
>
> Matt 13:38

The Johnsons were good people. They began to attend the church a few years ago, and, given their open personalities, it was easy to see that they just 'fit right in'. They attended church every Sunday, morning and evening, and were always present for mid-week Bible study on Wednesday evenings. They knew all the songs, and had a ready answer to any question, complete with the applicable scripture reference, whenever the principles of the Kingdom of Heaven were under discussion. It wasn't long before they were considered as candidates for leadership roles within the local body of Christ, which they reluctantly accepted with overt humility. Still, when the topic of discussion turned to a lifestyle totally committed to the furtherance of the gospel, separated from the defilement of worldly concepts, there was an uneasiness that soon became evident. It was then that the admonition to *"Judge not, lest you yourselves be judged"* became the end of all discussion.

There came a day in the life of the Body when the Spirit of God began to move upon His people in response to the fervent prayers of the pastor and two of the board members. The worship services were filled with hymns and songs that cried out to God for a more intimate union with the Creator, and the sermons became platforms for calling God's people to a lifestyle of holiness and sanctification. As the Body began to hunger and thirst after righteousness, God began to fill His people with a spiritual enthusiasm that had not been previously evident. Sunday morning services took on a whole new meaning, often lasting until well after the normal 12:00 noon dismissal time. Consequently, with a tinge of disgust, Mrs. Johnson apologized to the family for the dried-out Sunday roast that she set before them for the third time in three weeks. Not even the routine prayer of thanksgiving for God's bountiful provision could prevent the tirade concerning the need to be sensitive to the 'desires of the people', and the 'diversity of personal schedules'.

Week after week, while the majority of the Body reveled in the glory of the presence of God, the Johnson's grew increasingly critical of the direction that the Church seemed to be taking. Soon, what began as a mild resistance to the reforms that were happening, turned to open hostility toward the leadership. Seeds of suspicion, mingled with overt deception began to wield some telling blows to the very foundation of the body. Before long, it became increasingly evident that the members of the body were aligning themselves with different factions. There were those that became sympathetic to the oft-repeated arguments made by the Johnson's concerning the direction that the church was taking, and there were some who joined the pastor in his desire to discover a deeper walk with his Lord.

Tares—a plant that so closely resembles wheat—in fact, unless it is exposed to close scrutiny, even the trained eye may mistake it for the real thing. In the process of maturing, the two plants can grow side-by-side without anyone being aware of the differences. There comes a time, however, in the advanced stages of maturity, that it becomes evident that everything is not always what it appears to be. The most obvious difference between the two types of vegetation, is the fact that the tares do not bear edible fruit. While the wheat matures, and is used to produce one of the basic foods known to man, the tares, in a mature state, are totally worthless to the sustaining of life. In His teaching, Jesus identified the tares as the sons of the evil one. So often, they appear in the Kingdom of Heaven, and to the untrained eye, there seems to be little or no difference between them and the sons of the Kingdom. The real test comes when, under the scrutiny of God, they are examined for the fruit which they bear. The real wheat—the sons of the Kingdom—will be evident by their fruit, while the tares are conspicuous by their lack of fruit.

The difference becomes evident in the early stages of maturity. It didn't take long for the landowner's hired help to discern that something was definitely amiss in the field. Long before the actual harvest time, they were able to determine that, in addition to the desirable yield of valuable wheat, the field was also interspersed with undesirable, worthless tares. And so it happens, Jesus taught, that it doesn't take long before the sons of the evil one become evident in the Kingdom. *By their fruit you shall know them*, Jesus said of the sons of the Kingdom. Conversely, by their lack of fruit, the sons of the evil one become apparent.

In their indignation, the initial reaction of the hired help was to request leave of the Landowner to extract the tares from the presence of the good seed. It would seem a reasonable suggestion, given the undesirable qualities of the tares. And such is the response of many modern-day workers in the Kingdom of heaven as soon as the tare-like qualities of the sons of the evil one become evident. *"Let's root up the tares—let's expose them for what they are, and let's isolate them from the good seed."* Interestingly, the reaction of the Landowner to such a radical solution was one of logical caution. Rather than being overly concerned with the embarrassment of the subterfuge of the enemy, the focus of the Landowner was on the welfare of the good seed. *'No' he decided, 'for while you are gathering up the tares, you may uproot the wheat with them.*

In an honest self-evaluation, many of us would identify with the indignation of the workers, as well as their initial proposed solution. Having recognized the potentially harmful entities within the Kingdom, our first reaction is to begin rooting them out of the Body, thereby ridding ourselves of their effects. After prayerful consideration, however, we will often feel the check of the Holy Spirit in concern for the immature 'good seed'. How will our corrective efforts effect the growth of the sincere ones who desire to mature in the Kingdom of Heaven? To what extent are we liable to incur certain casualties in the remedial process? These are questions that will need to be answered on an individual basis in order to avoid incurring more injury to the Kingdom of Heaven.

Allow both to grow together until the harvest was the solution prescribed by the Landowner. Then, in the time of the harvest I will say to the reapers, "First gather up the tares and bind them in bundles to burn them up; but gather the wheat into my barn." Rather than risk incurring potential harm to the good wheat, a more conservative course of action was prescribed by the landowner. In fact, many of us would have interpreted such a solution as ineffective non-activity. The Landowner, however, was aware that, by harvest time, the wheat would be mature enough to withstand the process of separation from the tares. At that point, the tares were to be gathered first, bound in bundles, and burned in the fire. With little imagination, one can determine that the situation that Jesus is describing is what we have come to know as the 'final judgement'. Rather than taking the situation into our own hands, we would do well to follow the Landowner's solution of allowing 'spiritual tares' to grow alongside the true wheat until the day of judgement. At that day, the onus of judgement will be on the Righteous Judge who will recompense every man according to his deeds.

SHOPPING FOR THE BEST

"Again, the kingdom of heaven is like a merchant seeking fine pearls . . .

Matt 13:35

The five o'clock traffic was especially heavy tonight along the Cunningham By-pass. It seemed there must be some sort of obstruction ahead, judging from the ever-increasing jumble of hungry city-dwellers all heading home for supper. Jim Cheevers glanced impatiently at his watch—5:35—he probably wouldn't make it home now before The Six O'clock News started. The driver ahead of him didn't seem to notice that the light had turned green, so Jim felt obligated to bring it to his attention. A sharp blast of the horn seemed to bring the day-dreamer back to reality. Within minutes the reason for the traffic's delay became apparent when the flashing light brought his attention to the paramedics loading a stretcher into the back of the ambulance. A tow-truck was just raising a mangled sports-car on it's hook. It appeared that the car had engaged in an altercation with a lamp standard—a dispute which the car had lost.

"Some people's kids . . ." Jim muttered, as he followed the hand-signals of the traffic cop who was trying to make some sense of the flow of vehicles passing the scene. The ambulance driver turned on the flashing lights and wailing siren as he sped away from the scene in the opposite direction. "I wonder if it's anyone I know . . ." the familiar thought crossed Jim's mind as he guided the BMW back into the main flow of traffic. There it was again—that ever-invasive fear that always rose in his emotions whenever he witnessed any type of tragedy. With a quick shake of his head he mentally blocked any lingering thoughts that may have been dwelling in his sub-conscious.

Moments later, he was pulling the BMW into the wide drive-way of the ranch-style house at 1325 Fraser Avenue. The garage door responded to the remote control, and Jim eased the car into the wide, but cluttered, parking bay. The chirping of the burglar-alarm signaled his arrival to whoever was home, and the aroma of fresh-baked apple pie caused him to inhale in an extended manner. Jenny must have been baking again.

Jenny was the housekeeper he had hired soon after he won custody of eight year-old Carl, and five year-old Cindy. None of them were in sight just now—"probably in the back yard enjoying a splash in the pool" he thought. Jim stashed his briefcase in the small office just to the right of the master bedroom, and noted that the Six O'clock News would be starting in less than five minutes. It wasn't long before Jenny appeared to check on the supper.

"Oh, good-evening, Mr. Cheevers!" she always greeted him formally. "I didn't realize you were home. Supper will be ready in about five minutes. I'll just let the children know."

Jim settled down on the ample couch and chose the pre-programmed number on the television's remote-control device. When the announcer appeared on the screen, the lead story involved the mishap that he had witnessed on the way home from the office. Police had ruled that it was entirely accidental due to driver error, but no names had yet been released pending notification of next-of-kin. "Probably some young punk joy-riding in his dad's car," the words of his initial assessment replayed in Jim's mind.

"Hey Dad,!" the excited voice of young Carl interrupted his train of thought, and drowned out the next story on the news program, "can we play catch tonight?" He displayed the ever-present catcher's mitt that his Aunt Alice had sent him for his eighth birthday, and the softball that had been part of his mother's gift. Jim cringed inside—he had wanted to review that Polymar Investments portfolio tonight so that he could advise some of his clients who had been asking about it. Beside that, the news wouldn't be over until 7:00 p.m.

"Can we set that up for tomorrow, Sport?" he asked apologetically, "I really have a lot of work to do yet tonight." A stab of remorse hit him, as he witnessed the look of disappointment in his son's eyes, but what else could he do? He had to provide for his children, and that meant that he must keep his clients satisfied, and in order to do that, he had to be knowledgeable about the latest investment opportunities as they became available. "I'll tell you what," he suggested to the disheartened child, "tomorrow is Saturday. In the morning we'll go down to Rainbow Park—okay? Then we can spend a few hours perfecting that pitching arm!" Even Jim was getting excited about the prospect now.

"Yeah, OK", Carl agreed reluctantly. It was clear that his father's suggestion would do, but it wasn't exactly how he had planned it. He reluctantly made his way out the door to look for some of his friends, while his father returned to the conclusion of the Six O'clock News.

When the screen credits started to play, signifying the end of the newscast, Jim wandered into his office and retrieved the Polymar Investments portfolio from his briefcase. Closing the door to the office against any possible disruptions, he began to review the details of the prospectus. He had a solid client base that depended on him to bring them the highest returns, and he had built a reputation of being able to provide them with the best investment advice. So, what was this new opportunity all about anyway . . . ?

He was lost in his review when he heard a timid knock at the office door. "Yes . . . ?" he answered, again just slightly impatient at the interruption. Hesitantly, the door opened to reveal Cindy dressed in her nightgown, complete with her Book of Bible Stories tucked under her arm. Another birthday gift from Aunt Alice, it had become Cindy's most prized possession. The sparkle in those big innocent eyes, and the curls of auburn hair that fell just below her shoulders suddenly made the Polymar Investments prospectus seem of little importance. She sat, curled up next to him, as he opened the book and began to read about some man who had come to talk to Jesus in the middle of the night. At the end of the story, he closed the book and returned it to a sleepy-eyed Cindy. She replaced the book under her arm, and he hugged her and kissed her good-night, but she continued to stand in front of him.

"Good-night, Cinderella," he used his pet name for his daughter, expecting her to take her leave, but she remained fixed to the floor.

"Aunt Alice says we should talk to Jesus at night too!" she informed him.

"Oh brother, thanks a lot Alice!" he thought in his frustration. Now what was he supposed to do? Cindy seemed to pick up on his reticence. Without further hesitation her little hands reached for his, she closed her eyes tightly, and began to 'pray' in all her five-year-old innocence.

"Dear Jesus, please bless Mommy and Daddy, and please make them like each other again . . , and please keep all the bad men out of my room tonight . . ." After a number of similar child-like requests, when she finally said "Amen", Jim was totally speechless. He vaguely remembered hugging Cindy one last time and kissing her on her cheek, but after she left the room, he was lost in his thoughts. It felt like he had been punched in the belly! He had never realized that the effects of the divorce were still plaguing his children, and Cindy had never told him that she was having nightmares! He had always prided himself on being able to 'read' other people, but he had failed to understand the mental workings of his own offspring. The memory of Carl's disappointment at his refusal to 'play catch' was like a second left-hook He had made a career of assessing the value of monetary investments for his clients. So how could he miss the 'value' of investing time in interacting with his son?

The words from the story of Nicodemas' encounter with Jesus haunted him. "Are you a teacher of Israel, and yet you do not understand these things?" Maybe tonight Jesus could say to Jim Cheevers—"Are you an Investment Counselor with Midland Securities—but you miss cashing-in on the most valuable investment opportunities in your life?"

His thought was interrupted by the sound of the doorbell. Alice Cheevers stood at the door with her Living Bible in her hand. "I don't quite know how to say this", she offered sheepishly, "but the Holy Spirit told me that you needed someone to talk to tonight . . ." As the discussion unfolded, Jim told her about the impressions he had experienced after he read the story to Cindy. Alice found the text in her bible and read from the third chapter of John. Some of the verses Jim recognized from his childhood experience with Sunday School but had never really understood them. Alice patiently answered his questions and explained to him the different concepts that Jesus was trying to teach Nicodemas that night so long ago. Phrases like *For God so loved the world that he gave His only son . . .* along with *For God did not send his Son into the world to condemn the world . . .* took on a meaning that Jim had never before considered.

Before she left, Alice asked if he would consider one more verse. For the time she had spent he felt obliged to agree. She turned the pages and began to read: *Again, the kingdom of heaven is like a merchant, seeking goodly pearls: Who, when he had found one pearl of great price, went and sold all that he had, and bought it.* Yes, that was pretty much the story of Jim Cheevers' life—always seeking the very best—yet never really being satisfied with what he found. Expensive houses, fine cars, lucrative employment income, nothing had really satisfied his quest to succeed. His marriage was a failure, his parenting skills were largely unsuccessful,—but maybe he had just discovered the One Priceless Pearl . . .

Unlike the man who simply stumbled across the treasure hidden in the field, the merchant of pearls knew what he was looking for. He had made a career out of dealing in high quality merchandise, but was never fully satisfied with his wares. Regardless of where his quest led him, he always believed that there was something better. Lesser quality goods brought temporary satisfaction, but, sooner or later, he again succumbed to the desire for something better. In this illustration by Jesus, we see the reflection of the experience of many subjects in the kingdom of heaven. The more expensive substitutes, such as possessions, social status, reputation—all of them give some measure of temporal satisfaction, but, at the end of the day, the seeker is still unfulfilled.

Into the void, left by the dissatisfying quest, we can bring to them the Kingdom of Heaven. Although the circumstances surrounding the discovery of the pearl were so very different from those involving the hidden treasure, the responses to the discovery were identical. In both cases, the bottom line resulted in a complete liquidation of all other assets in order to acquire the prize possession. Again we are faced with the necessity of being totally 'sold-out' to the cause of acquiring possession of the One who is worth more than anything we have previously accumulated in our lives. Only after such a daring move can we live in the contented state for which we have given all of our previous efforts.

SEPARATING THE CATCH

"Again, the kingdom of heaven is like a dragnet cast into the sea, and gathering fish of every kind;
                                                                    Matt. 13:47

Braden Community Christian Fellowship church was set on a hill overlooking the small logging community from which it derived its name. It wasn't a particularly impressive building, but, with the rough log construction, it blended into its surroundings. 'Pastor' John Hawkins was employed by Green Valley Forest Products Ltd. as a first-aid attendant for five days each week, and fulfilled his pastoral duties each Sunday. In addition to those duties, he was often called upon to pray for the sick, counsel the confused, visit the widows, and provide leadership for the fledgling flock of believers. It wasn't surprising then, that Saturdays were jealously guarded islands-of-time at the end of a busy week.

The morning sun reflected off the windshield of the minivan parked in the driveway, lending a surreal glow to the bedroom wall, as John Hawkins hesitantly opened one eye. The digital alarm clock on the night table by the bed indicated that the time was 7:32 AM. A wave of panic threatened to overwhelm him until the realization dawned upon him that it was Saturday. Turning slightly to the left, the reassuring sight of Sandra's auburn hair on the pillow next to him filled him with a sense of joyful peace. Her shoulders rose and fell in a slow rhythm, indicating that she was still enjoying the extra hour of sleep. Silently, John breathed a prayer of gratitude to their Heavenly Father for the joy and the strength of their relationship.

The ringing telephone broke rudely into his reverie, and he scrambled to answer it in time to prevent Sandra from awakening. The breathless voice of Jake Windsor, the logging superintendent, didn't waste any time with formalities. "John, we've got a situation about twenty kilometers north of town, just off the Green Valley Mainline," he panted, "we'll need some first-aid coverage up there today. There's a crew-bus leaving the martialing yard in about forty-five minutes. Make sure you're there on time!" The line went dead, leaving John momentarily confused. When he collected his thoughts, he realized that Sandra was standing in the doorway to the bedroom, still trying to wipe the last traces of sleep from her eyes. The look on her husband's face told her that this would not be another lazy Saturday morning.

The next few minutes were lost in the mad scramble to meet the superintendent's directive. He took a hasty shower, while Sandra hurriedly packed his lunch-kit and made a few slices of toast. He quickly finished the toast that she had prepared, and drank the cup of microwave-heated coffee, as he briefly explained to Sandra the reason for his distress. As usual, she fully understood, and assured him that she would 'do just fine' in his absence. John mumbled a hasty prayer while they locked in a lingering embrace. With that, he was out the door and on his way to the martialing yard.

Most of the crew was already present when John parked the minivan beside the first-aid shack. A quick set of instructions was given before the men scrambled into the two crew-buses destined for the scene of action. John knew that he would probably see some of these men at church tomorrow—providing they could conquer the fire today—and he silently said a quick prayer for the safety of all the passengers leaving the yard.

The Chev Suburban, parked behind the first-aid shack, served as the logging crew's "ambulance". As John approached, he could see that his assistant, Ken Sterling, had already prepared it for the day's use. Ken was always amiable, but kept a certain distance whenever the two men had to work together. Ken and his wife, Sharon, were both members of 'the flock', but, while Sharon threw everything she had into serving her Lord, Ken remained somewhat aloof. It wasn't that he was openly hostile to the gospel message, in fact, his record of attendance and giving were impeccable, but there was no denying the hesitance in Ken's demeanor when deeper spiritual matters were under discussion. Today, however, the common threat of danger caused any differences to be temporarily abandoned.

They set up the first-aid station about three kilometers from the fire line, and listened to the portable radio as Jake Windsor gave orders and received updates of the situation from the various crews in the area. The fire was quickly advancing to a valuable stand of timber not far from the outskirts of the town. Heavy-equipment operators were working to build a fireguard between the flames and the edge of town. A look of concern passed between the two listeners as they realized that the area was not too far from where Ken Sterling's house was situated. Before they had a chance to spend any time discussing the potential danger, the radio reported the arrival of the first casualty. One of the younger members of the crew had suffered skin-burn due to his close proximity to the open flames. The situation occupied John's attention for some time, but when he returned to listen to the drama, he noticed the increased consternation on Ken's face.

"They're starting to evacuate our end of town!" Ken announced before John had a chance to ask for an update. "I hope Sharon and the kids will be alright!" John could detect the rising fear in Ken's voice.

"Why don't we pray about it, Ken?" The words were out of John's mouth before he had much time to consider what to say to the frightened younger man. Though he obviously felt a little foolish, Ken nodded numbly in agreement to the suggestion. Putting his arm around Ken's shoulders, John began to pray fervently. The drone of a water-bomber passing overhead caused John to pause momentarily, but as the sound faded he continued to pray for the safety of Ken's family and possessions, as well as for the safety of the rest of the town. The squawking radio again drew their attention to prepare for other incoming casualties. Still praying silently, John applied a thick layer of ointment to the foot of a crewmember who had inadvertently stepped into a burning sink-hole. As Ken applied the gauze dressing, the distant look in his eyes assured John that his younger assistant was also considering the power of prayer as the answer to the situation.

Again, the drone of another water-bomber drowned out the sound of the radio, but when they could again make out the words being communicated, a look of pleasant surprise passed between the two men. In the interim period since they last had their attention on the radio, it seemed that the wind had shifted and the danger to the town was no longer such a crisis. The effect of the air battle on the fire was beginning to produce positive results. Ken shook his head incredulously, pointing upward with raised eyebrows. John could only grin and nod affirmatively, as the realization of the power of prayer continued to register in the mind of the younger believer.

It was Sunday morning, and Braden Community Christian Fellowship appeared to be blessed with a larger-than-usual attendance. Ken Sterling sat in the aisle seat of the third row with his right arm draped lazily around Sharon's shoulder. It had been four weeks since the potentially disastrous fire had threatened the small town, and for the fourth consecutive week Ken sat and listened with rapt attention, as 'Pastor' John Hawkins opened his bible and began to read the text for the morning's sermon.

Again, the kingdom of heaven is like unto a net that was cast into the sea, and gathered of every kind . . . So shall it be at the end of the world, the angels shall come forth, and sever the wicked from among the just, and shall cast them into the furnace of fire . . . Memories of the raging inferno from which he and his family had been rescued flitted across Ken's mind as he pondered the fate from which he had been delivered—physically, as well as spiritually.

The kingdom of heaven is like a net. The net gathers fish of every kind. Still, within the net, there are "good" fish and "bad" fish. The contrasting words do not apply to quality as much as they do to utility. The word good may be better translated as 'useful', while the term bad would be closer to the English word 'worthless'. Given these definitions, it may be easier to understand Jesus' teaching concerning the kingdom of Heaven. Without too much effort we can identify the useful fish that can be found in the net of the Kingdom. These are the ones that desire to be utilized in the work of the Kingdom, giving of themselves for the purpose of feeding the spiritually hungry. Similarly, we could probably identify some worthless fish that we have met. Their mere presence in the 'net' does not guarantee their quality, and sooner or later, their worthlessness becomes evident. If the dividing line does not become apparent in this life, Jesus predicted, then certainly it will become evident at the end of the age. The notion of a separation process at the end of time should be a sobering concept to any member of the Kingdom. It should motivate us to consider our daily walk, and seek the guidance of the Holy Spirit in all aspects of our spiritual lives.

RECONCILING ACCOUNTS

"For this reason the kingdom of heaven may be compared to a king who wished to settle accounts with his slaves . . .
Matt 18:23

When it came to being shrewd in the business realm, Robert Fletcher was among the best—at least that was what the citation on his office wall declared. He had worked hard for the past twenty years to rise to this position, and his business colleagues still admired his prowess. Not only had the national office recognized his outstanding ability, but the local Chamber of Commerce had also given him the honor of electing him as their current president. But he certainly had not accomplished all of these things by his own knowledge or strength. Bob Fletcher would be the first to concede to anyone, that he could do nothing in his own strength, and that his success in the business world was the direct result of the grace of Almighty God.

There were times when his Christian testimony was something of an embarrassment to his business colleagues, but there was no doubt that ultimately, they respected him for his stand. Most people, who were aware of his story, were amazed at the changes that had occurred in his life in the past five years. There was a time when his success was the result of business tactics that would almost be considered as 'ruthless', but that was before he had *'found the Lord'*. Actually, Bob took every opportunity to remind people that, more correctly, it was a matter of the Lord finding him—after all, he would explain, 'it wasn't the Lord who had been lost'. In spite of the semantics, no one could deny that Bob Fletcher was indeed a new creation in Christ Jesus.

Certainly, life had not been easy for him. In his younger years, Bob could remember being placed in five different foster homes before he reached the age of eighteen years. He had never known his natural parents, although he understood that as a result of their continuing battle with alcohol, his grandmother had raised him for the first three years of his life. Problems with her health had forced her to seek the help of Social Services, and so, Bobby Fletcher had become a ward of the government. The majority of his adolescent years had been a time of emotional struggle, as he endeavored to gain acceptance from his peers. His quest for recognition had caused him to do some pretty stupid things in his high school years, even to the extent of obtaining a minor police record for auto theft and vandalism. Later in life he had applied for and obtained a pardon from the Justice Department, so that the foolishness of his younger years would no longer be a liability to him.

In his college years he had pursued an education in the field of business administration, and had been more than successful in his endeavors. Upon graduation, he had obtained employment with a major accounting firm, and later had accepted an offer of employment from one of the firm's clients. During those years he had met, and grew to love, Colleen—the boss's daughter, and it was about that time that he had accepted an invitation from the boss to attend a Full Gospel Businessmen's convention. Never being one to swallow anything hook-line-and-sinker, Bob spent the next several months examining the claims of Christ on his life. The idea of pardon, and absolution of guilt were nothing new to Bob, but he had never thought of those concepts in the light of eternity.

Ultimately, there came the day when the weight of the evidence was impossible to ignore, and Bob Fletcher received the word of grace with great joy. Since then his daily motivation had been to spread the good news about what God had done in his life. It seemed that no one could spend any significant amount of time with Bob before they heard the details of his life-changing encounter with Jesus Christ.

Today, Bob and Colleen Fletcher walked hand-in-hand down Barrows Street on their way to the bank, when a disheveled form of a man placed himself in their path. His eyes were bleary, and he tottered slightly as he held out a scarred hand for Bob's attention. "Excush me Shir," he slurred, "would you have an extra dollar to help a fella out? I haven't ate shinsh yeshtrday". Without a word of acknowledgement, Bob tightened his grip on Colleen's hand and drew her forcibly past the man until they were some distance down the street.

"Yeah, right!" Bob mumbled when they were out of earshot of the man. "So, go get yourself a decent paying job like the rest of us have to do!" Colleen glanced at him with one eyebrow raised as she usually did when she questioned the wisdom of his actions. "Well, it's true, isn't it?" he defended himself against her silent rebuke. "If he wasn't in the bottle so much, he would probably be able to work for his meals, and doesn't the Bible even say that if a man doesn't work he shouldn't eat?" Colleen had heard the argument countless times before, so she shrugged her shoulders in acquiescence, and they walked on together.

Emerging from the bank, they came face-to-face with Marcie Wheeler. Marcie was a recently converted single mother who, at the counsel of her social worker, had given her two-year old baby for adoption. Three years later, she still struggled with the consequences of her actions, though she had found some release from the Accuser's condemnation in the love and forgiveness of the Body of Christ.

"Marcie! So good to see you!" Colleen greeted the younger sister with exuberance. The next few moments were filled with the joy of Christian fellowship between Marcie and Colleen. Bob let the two women talk excitedly about the upcoming church dinner, while he waited patiently for the encounter to end. After several minutes, the women's conversation concluded with Marcie saying good-bye, while Bob and Colleen continued on their way.

"She sure seems cheerful," Bob commented, as they approached their parked car. Colleen detected just a hint of sarcasm in his voice.

"She certainly has a right to be cheerful!" Colleen affirmed, "considering all that she has been through in the last three years. Isn't it just awesome how the mercy of God can change lives that were so devastated by the effects of sin?" The concept made Colleen's eyes dance and sparkle with a vibrancy that Bob had always found so refreshing. Still, Bob couldn't help contemplating the future emotional pain of another little boy that would be raised not knowing the security of his natural parents' love.

The lack of his ability to rejoice with Marcie in her spiritual freedom became a source of consternation within Bob's spirit over the next few days. Furthermore, he repeatedly found himself considering the encounter with the drunken vagrant. Why were the two situations so repulsive to him? When he was really honest with himself, he was able to clearly detect a pattern of resentment toward other people caught up in similar lifestyles. The more he considered the dilemma, the more confused he became. Bob could usually share his story of God's love toward him with anyone who would listen—still, there were definitely classes of people to whom he found it impossible to relate. Discussing the problem with

Colleen, they decided that it was too big to try to resolve on their own. Without a doubt, they would need an objective third party to help them with this one. With that in mind, Bob made an appointment with their pastor, Glen Pearson, to discuss the matter with him.

Glen Pearson was a tall, slender man in his mid forties. He was married to Angela, and they had three children, ranging in ages from twelve to eighteen years. He was an easy-going individual, and was clearly comfortable to talk to. Most of his congregation had benefited from his wise counsel at various times of crisis in their lives. Now, as he approached Bob and Colleen from behind his desk, he paused to greet each of them with a short, but heartfelt embrace. He motioned for them to be seated, then led in a short prayer, inviting the Holy Spirit to be present, and to bless them with His wisdom and strength.

After a few introductory remarks, Bob found himself spilling the feelings of his heart to Pastor Glen, who listened politely, occasionally asking for clarification on certain points. Bob explained the disdain he felt for the drunken man on the street, as well as the difficulty he had experienced in rejoicing with Marcie. Soon, he found himself groping for any more words. To his surprise the pastor's first words addressed none of the situations that Bob had spent the past twenty minutes explaining. Instead, he looked at Bob with compassionate eyes, and simply asked, "Bob, what can you tell me about your parents?"

Bob was somewhat startled at the question. He questioned the connection between the pastor's question and their present discussion. At the same time, he definitely remembered sharing parts of his testimony with Pastor Glen on more than one occasion. Still, in the interest of co-operation, he began to relate his childhood experiences. Some parts were still painful to talk about, discussing the feelings of rejection experienced by little Bobby Fletcher some forty years prior. At times, he felt the comfort of Colleen's hand placed over his own, and he knew that she was praying for him. By the time he fell silent once again, he was embarrassed to find that his eyes were wet with tears, and that Colleen was patiently holding a Kleenex toward him.

"Don't be ashamed, Bob," he heard the encouraging voice of Pastor Glen, and felt the comforting hand on his shoulder. "This afternoon, God wants to heal the scars on Bobby Fletcher's heart . . ." Bob felt like someone was gently wrapping a comfortable blanket around his shoulders, as he listened to the pastor pray for the healing of his deepest emotions. Finally, the prayer was finished, and the three of them sat in silence, drinking in the refreshing feeling of freedom.

When the wonder of the moment subsided, Pastor Glen reached for his Bible and, after finding the scripture that he sought, he began to read. "For this reason the kingdom of heaven may be compared to a king who wished to settle accounts with his slaves . . ." As the pastor explained the relevance of the scripture, Bob began to realize that his disdain for the drunk man was the result of his inability to forgive his alcoholic parents. His problem relating to Marcie stemmed from his own feeling of abandonment by his mother. He saw, for the first time, the depth of the pit from which he had been dug, and the extent of forgiveness that had been extended to him by his Heavenly Father, in light of the pardon that he had withheld from those who had caused his childhood pain. A wonderful sense of release overwhelmed him when, at the prompting of Pastor Glen, he verbalized, "Mom and Dad," (he had never thought of addressing them with such familiarity) "I forgive you for abandoning me when I needed you the most . . ."

True forgiveness is ours, Jesus taught, when we are able to burn the record books. Often we are unaware that we still carry old accounts on our ledgers that are results of debts incurred by others years before. This is not to deny the validity of the 'debt'. Simply pretending that such a liability does not exist is only preparing for more trouble at some future time. Forgiving, Jesus taught His disciples, is an act of the will. Because of the sinful nature of man, there is no one who does not need to be forgiven, but, by an act of Father God's will, forgiveness was provided for all men. Similarly, we are all vulnerable to being offended by our fellow man. The debts caused by such offences are ours to resolve.

One course of action would be to simply write-off the debt, as the landowner did in Jesus' parable. Undoubtedly, we can recognize this situation as an example of the depth of Father God's mercy to each of us. Nothing we could do in our own strength would absolve us from our guilt. Still, because of God's love demonstrated by the death of His Son, we have become debtor's to His grace. The debt caused by our sin has been fully paid through the shed blood of Jesus Christ, and, when we appropriate that truth, God nullifies the balance on our account. Because of the prime example provided by God, we also need to follow His actions in our relationships with our fellowman.

The alternative to such action would be to demand retribution from the debtor, as the servant in the parable did to his fellow-servant. Clearly, this is not the course of action taken by Father God. but this is often the behavior exhibited by our humanity. Forgetting the pit from which we have been dug, so often we demand full recompense from those who are indebted to us. Such actions serve only to incur God's disapproval toward us, and may often bring a similar judgement upon our own heads. "Blessed are the merciful," Jesus said, "for they shall obtain mercy."

ANTICIPATING PAYDAY

"For the kingdom of heaven is like a landowner who went out early in the morning to hire laborers for his vineyard.
Matt 20:1

"It's not fair!" eleven-year-old Julie wailed, "Donny only dried three dishes, and he gets to go for ice-cream too?!" The implied inequity of the situation was clear to everyone within hearing distance—including Donny.

"But I did what Mom told me to do!" in all of his eight-year-old innocence, Donny defended himself from his sister's rebuke.

"Julie, that will be enough," Mary Sidney cut-off any further argument from the irritated Julie. "Each of you did what I asked you to do—and you both deserve a special treat. So why don't you get organized and we'll be on our way." There was no further discussion as the two children raced to obey their mother's latest directive. The prospect of the promised treat quickly became the central focus of their attention, and soon any thought of disparity was forgotten in the anticipation of the forth-coming pleasure.

The local 'Cone-Zone' Ice Cream Palace had a customer line-up extending to the door, as it usually did at 7:00 P.M. on a warm summer evening, and, as usual, Dave Donahue, the proprietor, was in a jovial mood. When it was finally their turn, he greeted the family, and took their order with his characteristic exuberance. Having responded to Dave's friendly chatter, and paying for the goods, Mary herded the two children out the door, and they headed in the direction of home.

"He's funny!" Julie observed as she licked an errant drip from her walnut-swirl cone. Mary was thankful they were some distance from the 'Palace' when Julie made her candid remark. There were times when Mary had made a similar comment to herself, though with a slightly different connotation. In fact, there were times she had to admit that Dave's slightly frivolous attitude was downright irritating. But then, she often found herself conceding, it wouldn't be that hard to act so jovial if one had the seemingly uncomplicated experience that was evident in Dave's life. As far as her own life was concerned, it wasn't easy raising two adolescent children by herself. Involuntarily, her mind flitted back to the joy she had shared with Raymond.

Next month, on the 'twenty-third', it would be six years since the solemn police officer had appeared on her doorstep to regretfully inform her of the fatal accident. Suddenly she found herself a single-parent to two lively youngsters, but God had been so faithful through all of her trials. How she thanked God for people like Ann Saunders who didn't mind just listening to the overflow of her raw emotions, or Mike and Diane Kearney, who would often take the children on an 'outing', along with their own four, just to give her some respite. Without the support of those people, and others like them, she couldn't imagine how she would have survived. How grateful she was for their solid support—but then there were the Dave Donahues of life who had never, or so it seemed, suffered any of the adversities of life that had afflicted herself and other members of the 'Body'.

"Good-night, Mommy," Julie's voice broke into her reverie, as Mary suddenly realized the girl had been standing, watching her quizzically for some time. Before she could respond, Donny appeared from the hallway with his Bible tucked under his arm. It was time for "devotions", a time of reading God's word, praying as a family for any pressing concerns affecting any or all of them. Often, it turned into a forum for discussion concerning some aspect of life, which the children found difficult to understand. There certainly had been plenty of those discussions since Raymond's death, often amazing Mary at the spiritual depth that the tragedy had brought to the children's lives. *"Out of the mouths of babes . . ."* Mary thought as she opened the Bible to the place where the black ribbon 'marker' was situated.

For the kingdom of heaven is like a man that is a householder, which went out early in the morning to hire laborers into his vineyard . . . Mary listened to the words as she read about the servants who were treated with equality by the householder, regardless of what hour of the day they had been hired. She had to admit that she had often found Jesus' statement puzzling when he stated—the last shall be as the first, and the first as the last. How could that be fair? The thought invoked the memory of Julie's frustrated statement from earlier in the day—"It's not fair!"

Mary closed the Bible and handed it back to Donny. In something of a fog, she was aware of praying with the children and kissing them goodnight before sending them off to have a good night's rest. Alone with her thoughts, her mind replayed a variety of scenes from the day, even as the words of the twentieth chapter of Matthew resounded in her memory. She was reminded of her own defense against Julie's veiled accusation earlier in the evening—*each of you did what I asked you to do*. Though the accomplishment had been different, the effort had been the same, she had no problem giving her children equal rewards for their obedience. She was tempted to be pleased with her spiritual insight, until the name 'Dave Donahue' was dropped into her mind.

Dave Donahue had appeared at church one Sunday about two years ago. His exuberance about life was his trademark, and everything he attempted seemed to be an automatic success story. He had only been a believer for about one year before he started coming to the church, but it was clearly evident that the blessing of the Lord was upon Dave's life. Perhaps it was the aspect of his recent conversion that caused Mary to regard his overt enthusiasm as a sign of spiritual immaturity. *But Dave can afford to be 'excited'*, Mary argued to herself, (or was it just to herself?). *He hasn't been through what some of the rest of us have had to endure. Wait until he has 'borne the heat of the day'*—where had she heard that phrase before?

Suddenly, it all became so clear to Mary. Undoubtedly, she had not been simply having an argument with her conscience. Rather, she had been defending herself against the conviction of the Holy Spirit. As the Light of Life illuminated the far recesses of her heart, she realized the extent of her pride, mixed with self-pity that had caused her aversion to Dave Donahue. The blessing of God that was evident in Dave's life in no way discounted the trial's she had borne. Did she really believe that she was entitled to a greater reward because of the trials that she had experienced? *But I did what Mom told me to* . . . Donny's defense presented the case for the blessings in Dave Donahue's life. The record showed Dave's faithfulness to God's calling on his life, even if it had only been a comparatively few short years. What right, then, had she to expect a greater reward for her efforts? With a trembling hand, Mary reached for her Bible and re-opened it to the twentieth chapter of Matthew. Tears ran down her cheeks, as she sought God's forgiveness for the hardness of her heart. With the calm reassurance that the ledger was clear on the Divine Records, she continued in a prayer of thanksgiving for the blessing that was evident in Dave Donahue's life.

In a society in which there is commonly a system of rewards based on achievement, it is not difficult to relate to Jesus' teaching in the first verses of the twentieth chapter of Matthew. This is one of those stark reminders of Jesus' words to Pontius Pilate when He said *"My kingdom is not of this world . . ."* We should not expect that our designation as a "long-time member" of the Kingdom will have any effect on the value of our eternal reward. Still, if we can honestly scrutinize our system of beliefs, we must admit that, even subconsciously, we often subscribe to such concepts.

In this parable that Jesus taught, we see four distinct groups of workers. There were those who stood in the marketplace at the first light of dawn, hoping to be hired for the work of the day. They anticipated the labor as well as the rewards, and were eager to get an early start on the day. For this group, the wages were defined, in advance, as 'a penny' for the day. It doesn't seem like much in today's economy, but for the day in which Jesus taught it was the commonly accepted daily wage. Here we observe a picture of many saints who, it seems, have 'always been believers'. Whether they enjoyed a Christian heritage, or whether they simply were 'in the right place at the right time' at a relatively early age, the majority of their lifetime has been spent as workers in the Kingdom.

Then, there were those that were discovered in the marketplace at the third hour. In today's reckoning of time, we would say that it was approximately 9:00 AM. They may well have been prepared to work at the crack of dawn like the others, but the increased demand for workers found them ready when they were needed most. Certainly, their eagerness was no less than their counterparts, who had already been at work for three hours by now, and they had no problem fitting into the flow of the workforce. In addressing the matter of the pay scale, we note that the landowner is not as specific with this group as he was with the Sunrise Crew. Rather than defining a specific amount, he simply agrees to pay them *'what is right'*, or *'just'*.

Similarly, at the sixth hour and the ninth hour, or approximately at noon and 3:00 PM, the landowner found himself in the marketplace seeking more laborers. The presence of workers still in search of meaningful employment at these later times did not seem to surprise the landowner. In keeping with his bargain made to the 'nine-to-fivers', the agreed rate of pay would be *'whatever is right'*.

It would seem that there was no shortage of work on the day in question, for, again at the eleventh hour, about 5:00 PM, the search was made for still more workers. Their availability seemed to puzzle the landowner, but, in response to his query, the profoundly simplistic reason given was *'because no one has hired us'*. Certainly, the record shows their willingness to be used, but, as the apostle Paul would say, *'they lacked opportunity'*. Again, the landowner was quick to seize the opportunity, fulfilling their desire to be 'hired', and promising to pay them 'whatever is right'.

When the workday had ended, it was time for the workers to receive their pay. Undoubtedly, the air was thick with anticipation as they were called into the paymaster's office. It must have been somewhat surprising, however, for the eager workers to find themselves arranged in 'reverse order' to their hiring schedule. But, no matter, they had waited this long for this moment—what difference would a few extra minutes make? When the swing-shift emerged from the pay office, each one sported a penny in his hand. A full day's wages for one hour's work!

Wait a minute! Wasn't that the amount of remuneration that had been promised to the Sunrise Crew? Whatever could the landowner be thinking?! That could only mean one thing—after some deliberation, the landowner must have re-thought his offer to the Sunrise Crew, and possibly to the Nine-to-Fiver's, and maybe even the Afternoon Shift. They must have all been awarded some sort of retroactive pay increase. Their hopeful faces soon turned to disappointment, however when all of them left the paymaster's table with a penny in their hand.

"It's just not fair!"—how many of us have heard, or even voiced that sentiment as workers in the Kingdom of Heaven? *"But he's just a brand-new Christian, Lord! Why—I've been serving You for over forty years now!"* And with many similar accusations we try to convince the Almighty of His lack of equity. *"I've suffered so much for You, Lord, and you make this babe-in-Christ equal to me?!"* We may not have voiced our feelings with those exact words, but if we can truly be honest with ourselves, many of us would have to admit that, at some point in our experience we have had a similar verbal exchange with the 'Heavenly Landowner'.

Many would find themselves shuddering at the blatant impudence of such a remark, but it didn't seem to bother the Landowner to any great extent. *"Friend"*, he addresses the sputtering worker calmly, *"I do you no wrong . . ."* Isn't it good to know that, even in the weakness of our humanity, the Master still calls us 'friend'? Gently, He reminds the workers of their original agreement, and reaffirms His right to reward each individual worker as He sees fit.

The wages of sin is death, Paul states, *but the gift of God is eternal life*. When we get right down to it, we have to admit that the only thing we have been promised as workers in the Kingdom of Heaven is eternal life. No one was ever promised anything more, and no one who is faithful will ever receive anything less. Even then, the final payment cannot, in any way, be construed as 'earned wages'. Rather, eternal life is nothing short of an outright *'gift of God, not a result of works, lest any man should boast'*.

SETTING THE TABLE

"The kingdom of heaven may be compared to a king who gave a wedding feast for his son.

Matt 22:2

Pastor Phil Barnett opened one eye and looked at the LED clock that stared at him from the nightstand. It was now 2:00 AM. The last time he had checked, it had read 1:48 AM. It promised to be a long night. He lay in the stillness listening to the measured breathing of his beautiful wife, Sonya, and wondered again how things had become so 'messed up'. Scenes from last night's Board meeting still haunted him, and the more he tried to put them out of his mind, the more vivid they became. *'Commit your way to the Lord . . .'* the same words that he had so often offered in counsel to those in his pastoral care, now echoed in his spirit. As he turned to find a more comfortable position, Sonya stirred, and muttered something unintelligible. Not wanting to awaken her completely, he silently slipped out of bed, determining to head downstairs to 'the den'.

'The den'—it seemed a fitting title for the place where he had spent considerable time in the past while. Many times he had waited in prayerful anticipation as the Adversary, like a roaring lion, had prowled through his tiny flock, seeking someone to devour. But for now, he retreated to a small corner of the basement, where he had invested much time and effort last winter installing the red cedar paneling. Completing the picture was the sandstone-colored shag carpet that he had purchased as a 'roll-end special' from Braun's Hardware Store in the Greendale Shopping Centre.

Pastor Phil, as he was called by the faithful of the flock, slumped into the padded chair behind the big oak desk that served as the altar of the Almighty at times like this. He hadn't wanted to burden Sonya with the details of last night's meeting before she drifted off to sleep, but he knew that she had sensed his spiritual weariness. Once again, he thanked God for her love and support before becoming engulfed in painful intercession for those who had been entrusted to his care. *My close friend in whom I trusted . . .* the words of the Psalmist bubbled in his mind . . . *has lifted up his heel against me . . .* For a moment he felt that he knew something of the pain that Jesus had experienced when He gave Judas Iscariot his leave from the supper table with the instruction to 'do what he had to do, and to do so quickly'.

It hadn't come as a complete surprise, as he reminisced about the events of the past year. There had been a number of 'warning signals', but Pastor Phil had always clung to the promise that God causes all things to work together for our good . . . However, things had come to a 'head' in the past month, leading to the announcement by Don Baker at the meeting last night that "the majority of the congregation no longer placed any confidence in his ministry". As he knelt beside the high-backed leather chair in his office, the emotions ran visibly down his cheeks. "Father, forgive them", his spirit groaned, "they don't know what they are doing". It seemed to be an eternity that he wrestled with the enemy of Discouragement, and, just when it seemed there were no more tears left to weep, he felt a soft hand being placed gently on his left shoulder. He turned slightly in response, almost expecting to see a heavenly visitor sent to comfort him, but the one who returned his gaze was his own little angel—Sonya.

The next few moments were spent in tearful communion, as Pastor Phil once again unburdened his heart to his best friend and closest confidant. The longer they talked, the more Phil felt the fear being replaced by the love that he shared with Sonya. How he thanked God for her unconditional love and solid support. After some time of silent unity, they found their way back to the kitchen, where Sonya proposed to brew some cinnamon tea.

"I ran into an old friend in the mall today . . ." Sonya began, trying desperately to change the topic to something less strenuous.

"I do hope you didn't hurt her . . ." the words were out of his mouth before he had a chance to think about them. Phil glanced at Sonya to judge her reaction to the quip, but her eyes only danced with relief at his humor. She proceeded to describe her encounter with Jenna Harmor. Jenna had been a foster child when she went to high school with Sonya about ten years prior. Her life in the intervening period had not been happy. After five years of a stormy marriage, her husband had deserted her, leaving two adolescent children for her to raise on her own. Though she had never been very heavenly-oriented, it had become clear, in the course of their conversation that Jenna was very tired of the agony of circumstance that had so recently engulfed her.

"I invited her to church on Sunday," Sonya concluded hesitantly, "but I don't know if she will actually be there."

"She'll come if she is hungry enough," Pastor Phil re-iterated the words that he had often used in comforting others in regard to unsaved friends and family. "What we need to do is to make sure that there is food on the table when she arrives." Pastor Phil surprised himself with the fervency of his last statement, but in his spirit, he knew that it was a word of wisdom to himself from Father God.

It was Sunday morning, and the sun had risen, as it usually did—even when the night seemed to be so dark. And with the sun, as usual, renewed hope dawned in the spirit of Pastor Phil Barnett. The horror of Thursday night's Board meeting seemed to be of even less consequence, as Phil and Sonya enjoyed a delicious breakfast of French toast and sausages. As far as the future of their ministry was concerned, they had conceded to leave the matter to God's wisdom to shut the doors that no man could open, and to open the doors that no man could shut. If this was where the Lord wanted to use them, they were content to stay—no matter what the Board decided. At the same time, they knew that if God was indeed shutting this door, He would open another one that no man could shut.

The time of praise and worship had been refreshing, but now it was time to satisfy the flock with the milk of the word, and the Bread of Life. Pastor Phil opened the Word to his chosen text for the morning, and read the first ten verses of Matthew 22. When he looked out at his congregation, he felt that he knew something of the emotions of the King. There were some that looked at him in expectation, others were more detached, as if they were simply fulfilling some spiritual obligation. Still others seemed almost hostile, as if daring him to speak a word out of turn. Near the back of the church, just behind Len and Janet Brown, a young woman sat by herself. Her hair was slightly disheveled, and her light blue bulky-knit sweater hung loosely over a pair of faded jeans.

Whenever his gaze happened to fall on her, the woman looked back at him expectantly. As Pastor Phil began to divide the word of truth with the small congregation, he noted that the newcomer was receiving the teaching with a child-like hunger. By the time the sermon was ended, the woman was visibly wiping the tears from her eyes. She appeared to be slightly embarrassed by her display of emotions, and Phil silently prayed that she would not leave before he had an adequate opportunity to talk to her after the service was concluded.

When the congregation had been dismissed, Pastor Phil made his way toward the back of the church. He was nearing the foyer when he heard Sonya's excited squeal. "Jenna! You came! It's so good to see you!" Phil turned to see Sonya locked in the embrace of the woman who had occupied the back pew. So that's who she was! It was obvious that Jenna was still struggling with her emotions, as Sonya introduced her to Phil. Without too much hesitation, Jenna accepted their invitation to dinner, and the two women talked excitedly during the short trip home. For the balance of the afternoon, Phil and Sonya ministered to the needs of Jenna's wounded spirit.

Soon, there were others that began to arrive at the table from all walks of life. It was surprising to Pastor Phil and Sonya to realize just how many hungry souls had wandered the highways and byways of their community for so long. In the midst of the rejoicing, there was a tinge of regret when Don Baker announced that he no longer desired to be a member of the board. Though it was certainly not the manner in which Pastor Phil would have chosen to resolve the matter, it was apparently the answer to his prayers for God's intervention.

The kingdom of heaven, Jesus taught, *is like unto a certain king, which made a marriage for his son* . . . Given our present-day knowledge of the scriptures, and in the light of history, it isn't difficult to see the intent of Jesus' teaching. The concept of the 'marriage supper of the Lamb' is one that strikes a chord of expectancy in the heart of any true believer. Still, in the eternal concept, we know that there is an air of 'aloofness' that is prevalent in today's society in general, and, sadly enough, within the 'church' in particular. In this age of 'instant' everything, the idea of waiting induces a sense of impatience within the majority of would-be believers. The fact that we have seen two thousand years of history since Jesus declared ' . . . *and if I go, I will return and receive you unto myself'*, appears to justify such a sentiment.

In the process of 'waiting', it is evident that over the centuries, mankind has responded in the same manner as the invited guests in Jesus' parable. Many of God's messengers, over the centuries, have been ignored, and some have even been beaten and mistreated by the 'invited guests'. Finally, in a desperate attempt to gain man's attention, God sent His only Son. *He came unto His own*, the prophet foretold, *and His own did not receive Him.* Instead, they accused Him, tried Him, convicted Him, and finally executed Him on totally false charges.

In a sobering concept, Jesus described the judgement that awaits those who have consciously rejected the invitations of the King. Because of the blatant dismissal of His invitation, there awaits a final judgement on those who were summoned to the Wedding Feast, but consciously refused to attend. However, the story does not end on a totally hopeless note. In the centuries that have passed since Jesus' resurrection, the call has been carried into the highways and byways of the world. Now, the guest-list includes the 'whosoever will' that hear and obey the invitation of the Father. Certainly, the question arises with every generation of believers as to the value, and the urgency of spreading the Good News. The obvious answer to such a query lies in the expression of the apostle John, that God is not willing that any should perish, but that all should come to repentance.

As a result of the extended invitation of the King, guests were gathered from all walks of life, as Jesus' described—both 'bad and good'. It is interesting to note that the original meaning of the word used for 'bad' extended not only to the immediate ethical sense of 'evil' or 'wicked', but also to a more subtle concept of *'being pressed or harassed by labors, annoyances, or perils'*. Using the more comprehensive meaning, it is evident that the invitation includes all of mankind, since there is none that would fall outside of such parameters.

Additionally, the invitation was extended to the 'good' people that could be found on the highways and byways. A closer examination of this word reveals a definition that included such concepts as 'useful', 'pleasant', 'agreeable', or 'distinguished'. In the light of such a concept we find a definition of what is probably the majority of the population in today's society. Yet, no matter how pleasant or agreeable they appear to be, they still need to hear the invitation to the banquet table.

In a slightly unusual addendum to the main theme, Jesus paints the picture of the guest who was found by the king lacking a 'wedding garment'. While others were waiting in excited anticipation, ready to enjoy the imminent pleasurable event, here stood one that was totally unprepared for the occasion. Certainly, he appeared to be a part of the crowd, but for the fact that he was dressed inappropriately. In an attempt to ascertain just how he came to be a member of the assembly, the king asks the simple question, Friend, how did you come in here without a wedding garment? The man had no reply to such a question.

Unfortunately, we are warned, there are going to be some surprised guests at the final banquet table. Jesus said that, in the final analysis, every man will have to give an account of himself. Those that have 'nothing to say' in that moment will be consigned to the 'outer darkness'. Such a concept should initiate a serious soul-search by all who have responded to 'the invitation'. *'Not everyone who says to me 'Lord, Lord' will enter into the kingdom of heaven'* Jesus said. May we never be found 'speechless' in the Heavenly receiving line when every man will have to give an account of himself.

EXPECTING THE GROOM

Then shall the kingdom of heaven be likened unto ten virgins, which took their lamps, and went forth to meet the bridegroom . . .

Matt 25:1

It was an oppressive hush that filled the little room. The only sound was the soft strains of a compact disk playing its music through the wall-mounted speakers. Thirty-two people sat in silence on cloth-upholstered metal chairs, each lost in their own thoughts and reminiscences. Tracy Crofton let the words of the background music fill her memory.

" . . . *So I'll cherish the old rugged cross* . . ." yes, that had been the essence of 'Mom's' life and testimony to the world. " . . . *'Til my trophies at last I lay down* . . ." Tracy could almost see her mother cautiously placing a richly jeweled container before the throne of her Savior and Lord. "*I will cling to the Old Rugged Cross* . . ." For as long as she could remember, Mom had been unashamed of the source of her spiritual strength and peaceful demeanor. " . . . *And exchange it someday for a crown* . . ." In her mind's eye, there was Mom, kneeling before a glittering throne, as two hands gently placed a diamond-studded tiara on her long, flowing, auburn hair. A sense of joy, mingled with the sorrow of the moment, gave rise to a fresh wave of emotion that ran unashamedly down her cheeks. For the next few moments, Tracy allowed herself the luxury of giving free expression to the grief that had been just below the surface of her emotions for the past number of weeks. They had all known that this hour was imminent, but that knowledge did nothing to diminish the sorrow of the moment.

Tracy fumbled with her small handbag that she carried, desperately searching for a fresh Kleenex. Her search was unsuccessful, and she almost panicked in her embarrassment, until a hand gently, but firmly, nudged her upper right arm. Turning slightly, she saw the necessary tissue being offered to her from the rugged hand of her older brother, Thomas. There he was again, just when she needed him the most. She gave him a weak, but grateful smile, and he nodded back at her with that strong, understanding half-grin.

The CD was playing the chorus once again, but this time Tracy's thoughts turned to Thomas. He appeared to be so emotionally stable, but Tracy sensed the turmoil in Thomas' spirit. No matter how much of a strong, masculine image he tried to portray, she knew that her brother was reaching his breaking point. Mom, and Thomas—they had always shared that special 'mother-son' relationship, but in the past few years, Thomas had wandered away from his mother's rock-solid faith. It seemed to have begun shortly after Dad's fatal accident, but Tracy knew that the problem had started long before. Now, with the loss of both parents, she had the feeling that the responsibility of her brother's spiritual life had fallen upon her shoulders. "Dear God, give me strength . . ." she muttered through her tears, just before the pastor's voice called her abruptly back to the stark reality of the moment.

The balance of the afternoon was spent in a numb sensation of half-reality. She was aware of Thomas' strong arm supporting her as they watched the delicately-crafted casket being lowered into the freshly dug plot beside their father's monument. Again, she drew from his strength, while the women of the church served a light lunch of sandwiches and tea to the small group gathered in the fellowship hall. Inevitably, however, the time of fellowship came to an end, and Thomas walked her to his waiting rental car in the church parking lot. They had agreed that they would spend the night at 'the house' before Thomas' return flight to Vancouver the following day.

The familiar rooms held many pleasant memories for both of them. The normal family banter was absent tonight, but the reminders of their parent's rock-solid faith were present everywhere. The walnut-stained cross that Dad had fashioned in the shop still hung on the wall above their parent's bedroom door. The cross-stitched canvas displaying the empty tomb, with the words "He is risen, indeed!" was still in its place above the floral-patterned love-seat. As if to complete the picture, the old, leather-covered family Bible lay open on the cedar-toned coffee table in front of the matching floral-patterned sofa. The scenario held so many memories for both of them as they sat in the holy hush of the room.

Nodding towards the open bible, Tracy broke the awesome silence. "Read to me, Thomas ?!" the request of the 'little-girl Tracy' from twenty-five years prior tumbled from her mouth. A look of mutual recognition flashed across his face, as Thomas clumsily reached to retrieve the volume from the table in front of him. Unsure of just where to start, he let his eyes fall to the page where the Bible lay open, and began to read the first words that he saw.

"Then shall the kingdom of heaven be likened unto ten virgins, which took their lamps, and went forth to meet the bridegroom . . ." He began in a strong, masculine voice, but, as his reading progressed, his speech became husky with emotion. Finally, as Thomas read the Bridegroom's declaration *"Verily I say unto you, I know you not . . ."* the conviction became stronger than his will, and Thomas dissolved into tears of remorse. As Tracy reached to comfort her older brother, her mind wondered at the temporary reversal of roles. Throughout their lives, Thomas had always been the strong one, but now, she rose to the occasion, as it became evident that he needed to draw from her strength.

After a few hours of restorative communion, both siblings headed for their respective rooms with tears of joy still evident on their faces. Tracy was still awe-struck at the grace of God, and how the event of their mother's death could give birth to the 'new life' that her brother had finally found that evening. As she yielded to the heaviness of slumber, Tracy was sure that she heard the jubilant voices of both Mother and Father in their sweetest harmony. *" . . . I will cling to the Old Rugged Cross, and exchange it some day for a crown . . ."*

In the kingdom of heaven, Jesus explained, there will be those who are prepared, and some who are unprepared for the wait. The first-century Christians firmly believed that they would witness Jesus' return in their lifetime. Subsequent generations have thrived on similar expectations. History has revealed, however, that God's timetable is not necessarily equivalent to man's expectations. Twenty centuries later, we are still waiting for His promised return. Rather than diminishing from the reality of the promise, the extended period of time serves only to heighten the expectations of those who are faithful to His calling.

The bridegroom, in Jesus' story, had summoned all of the virgins to rejoice with him at the occasion of his wedding. In expectation of the joyful event, all of the virgin's responded to the invitation. There were, however, within the ranks of the invited, markedly differing levels of wisdom. The wise, Jesus stated, took extra oil in their flasks with their lamps. The foolish, on the other hand, made no provision for the chance that there may have been some delay in the bridegroom's schedule. Consequently, in the interim period, the inevitable happened. As everyone became weary with the wait, each of their lamps were extinguished for lack of fuel.

In a spiritual application of the principles that Jesus discussed, it is not difficult to identify the danger to every believer as we wait for our Bridegroom. Note that all of the young women that Jesus described had responded to the invitation. In like manner, each member of His church has received, and responded to the invitation to the Marriage supper. There is a distinction drawn, however, on the issue of preparedness among the invited guests. There were those that assumed that the proceedings were imminent, and made no provision for a potential delay. Others had the forethought to prepare for a possible postponement by carrying extra oil for their lamps in portable flasks.

As the evening progressed, Jesus explains, all of them became weary, and fell into an exhausted slumber. Note that the object of Jesus teaching was not the propensity to become weary of the wait. Surely, because God knows our human weaknesses, He accepts the fact that we will all, at some point in our Christian experience, become weary, and even tend to slumber at times. The line of distinction, however, was drawn at the point of the Bridegroom's approach. When the announcement of His coming was made, there was a mad scramble to prepare for his belated arrival.

Those virgins that were labeled as "wise" simply took the extra oil that they had brought and re-lit the smoldering wicks of their lamps until they shone brightly in expectation. The "foolish", however, were faced with the stark reality of their lack of provision for this moment. Their immediate solution was to turn to their wise companions, and beg their assistance in the time of crisis. How often have we been witnesses to such a mad scramble within the Kingdom of Heaven? Whether in our own experience, or the lives of fellow-believers, we can all remember times when circumstances of life have caught us totally off-guard, and left us scrambling for a solution to our dilemma. At that point it is a mark of wisdom to have a spiritual reserve upon which we can draw, to see us through the dark times. We find that spiritual stamina is not a commodity we can ask of others, it is a personal quality that each of us must possess for ourselves.

This is not to say that we should not expect spiritual support from the Body in times of crises. Certainly, such a luxury is one of the main benefits of being a member of the Body of Christ. Rather, the principle appears to be, as the Apostle Paul articulates, that every man must bear his own burden or obligation to the Kingdom. Without that spiritual reserve, such experiences will find us ineffectively seeking to draw from the spiritual stockpile of others.

When their fellow-guests were unable to help in their predicament, the foolish virgins took to the streets in search of common merchants to fulfill their desires. Is this not a sad commentary on the response of many in the kingdom in their time of spiritual need? The "merchants" are readily available, but they do not stock the commodity that is so desperately needed at such times. Unfortunately, while their search drew them away from the banquet hall momentarily, the Bridegroom arrived. Those that were faithfully waiting were invited inside, and the door was shut. When the wandering ones finally returned, prepared for the banquet, their harried cries for recognition went unacknowledged. The concept of finality is so sobering that it should cause all of us to do much soul-searching. Are we prepared for the wait that we may well experience as we anticipate the coming of the Bridegroom? If not, will our lack of preparation find us seeking solutions elsewhere when the Bridegroom does make his appearance? Do we dare to face the dire consequences of the closed door, if we are unable to correctly answer the previous questions?

Surely, today is the day to make adequate preparation for the arrival of the Bridegroom, so that, in that day, we will not be found wanting oil for our burned-out lamps.

ASSESSING THE RISK

For the kingdom of heaven is as a man travelling into a far country, who called his own servants, and delivered unto them his goods.

Matt. 25:14

There were times when Jerry Beamer could be downright irritating. What was his problem, anyway? Why did he always have to be so negative? "We've never done it that way before . . ." was always his ultimate defense. Peter Braden sat, silently fuming, reviewing his notes while the other members of the board carried on the animated discussion. Establishing a 'drop-in center' in the Sandhurst Industrial Park was certainly a radically new idea for the relatively small congregation, but, in discussion with other members of the board, Peter knew that there was a consensus of opinion indicating that it was definitely 'doable'. Still, Jerry Beamer pulled a lot of weight with the 'old school' members.

'Sandhurst Industrial Park' was a recently renovated low-cost housing development in the north-end of the city. Since it had been revamped, it had been renamed Sandhurst Estates but everyone still referred to the area by its original designation. Until five years ago, the area had been infamous for it's derelict warehouses among the abandoned railway yards. After a major fire destroyed three of the old structures in one night, the city council decided to redevelop the area in a manner that would help to solve the existing housing crisis. Regardless of the facelift, and the city's ad campaign declaring the virtues of urban revitalization, the district still carried the stigma of the past.

Pastor Harvey Bernatti had been raised in a similar environment, and, more recently, had been impressed with the need to establish an outreach into that community. Of course, the initial response was one of genuine fervor, but, in the past few months, the idea had drawn increasing criticism. Tonight, the pastor sat with his board, discussing the methods of achieving such an undertaking.

"Why should we be concerned about that area of the city? We've got enough to worry about just keeping our heads above water as it is. And just who do we expect to run this thing?" Jerry's voice was bordering on sarcasm.

"George Barker has offered to organize this operation for us", Pastor Harvey reminded him, "and with his experience, and his testimony, I believe that the Lord will bless him for his efforts."

"And not only that", Peter interjected with obvious excitement, "North-end Properties has offered us space in the old Macdonald Building for only one thousand dollars a month!"

For the first time that Peter could remember, Jerry Beamer was speechless. He looked at each of his comrades in turn, trying to detect a trace of humor on anyone's face, but all he saw was genuine sincerity. "George ?" Jerry finally sputtered, "what would George Barker know about a ministry like that? And a thousand dollars a month? Where is that going to leave us financially?"

George Barker was a relatively new addition to the body of believers. He was in his late twenties, his Sunday appearance was extremely casual, to say the least, and his personality was definitely laid-back. Some people thought he was almost frivolous, but Pastor Harvey knew that there was a spiritual depth and an evangelistic fervor to George that few people ever saw. As for the price-tag on the project, though it sounded risky, most people conceded that it could be done. When the final vote was taken, there were three affirmative votes, and one dissenting. And so it happened that Agape Center was birthed.

It was almost a year since the tension-filled meeting had occurred. A young man with shoulder-length hair, dressed in a fleece top and jogging pants, sat beside June and Keith Proctor, obviously comfortable with the time of praise and worship. June and Keith had been the first-fruits of the Agape Center outreach. In response to George Barker's patient ministry, their crumbling marriage had been repaired, and the Lord was evidently using their new-found love to give birth to still more 'babes in Christ'. Pastor Harvey was once again overcome with gratitude to God for His love and grace to the little flock. Agape Center had certainly proved to be a good investment, with visible returns in response to the fervent prayers of the faithful. As for Jerry Beamer, at the annual meeting, the congregation had not renewed his appointment to the board. In his place, George Barker had been installed as the newest board member, and continued to serve the Lord, as well as the congregation, in the new direction that God was leading His people.

For the kingdom of heaven is as a man travelling into a far country, who called his own servants, and delivered unto them his goods . . . In the parable that followed, Jesus taught his disciples a valuable lesson in stewardship. It is a parable that causes much soul-searching in an attempt to find the answer to the question—"What have we done with what we have been given?" We can understand the spiritual application, when we think of the differing levels of ability that the landowner recognized in each of his servants. They were not all entrusted with the same amount. Rather, Jesus said, they were each given according to their 'several ability'. Notice that the Master had already determined their ability, and fully expected that each of them would perform to their greatest potential. We often think that, within the Kingdom, everyone is on an 'equal footing'. Though Jesus taught that we are equal in our eternal value to the Kingdom, He did recognize that, in each of our lives, there are differing levels of individual capabilities.

Having assessed the capabilities of each of his servants, the landowner left them to their duties and went on a journey. Though no specific instructions were given, it is apparent that he fully expected each servant to act in a trustworthy manner during his absence. The one who had received the five talents proceeded to earn five more talents through his prudent efforts. Similarly, the one who had received the two talents was able, through practical endeavors, to produce two more talents. However, we know the story of the servant who had received only one talent.

Obviously, the object of the exercise was not to increase the wealth or social standing of the servants to whom the amounts were entrusted. Rather, the intent was to enhance the wealth of the master. Similarly, we can understand that the gifts that God gives to us in our present circumstances are definitely not for our personal advantage. They are to be used solely for the purpose of furthering, or adding increase to the kingdom of Heaven. Perhaps, knowing that he stood to make no personal gain in the effort, the servant who had received the lone talent determined that he was not going to make someone else rich from his own endeavors. The 'what's-in-it-for-me' mentality caused him to simply bury his lord's money in the backyard, waiting, unprofitably for the master's return. In a moment of self-examination, we should all, periodically, ask ourselves if such is not the rationale that often keeps us from acting to further the Kingdom of Heaven. Do we hesitate to take certain risks, realizing that, ultimately we stand to gain no 'special merit badges' for our efforts?

Indeed, the very heart of the servant is exposed in his defense to the master's scrutiny. *"I knew that you were a stern man . . ."* the servant begins, *". . . so here is what is really yours"*, as he hands the master only the amount of the initial investment. Can we detect a hint of accusation there? In his mind he has already judged his master's motives to be less than perfect. Because of his biased estimation of his master, he conducts himself in a manner that is in direct opposition to the purpose of his position. One could speculate that perhaps the master already knew the heart of his servant, and consequently limited the opportunities for the man. Certainly, if he had entrusted this man with the five talents, the master would have incurred a much greater opportunity loss. Whatever the rationale, it was apparent that this servant had proved himself to be untrustworthy.

"Even if you didn't want to assume the risk . . ." the master rephrases the servants defense, *"you should have, at the very least, put the money in the bank. That way I would have earned simple interest on my investment"*. It is sobering to think how many of us will hear only the Master's rebuke when it is revealed that we have taken what has been entrusted to us, and merely hid it in some inconspicuous corner of our lives. Rather than using it for the advancement of the Kingdom, and at least attracting the interest that builds up over such an investment, we have concealed His blessings in some 'spiritual safety-deposit box'. There it remains, without benefit to us, and totally unprofitable to the Kingdom of Heaven. Recognizing that *'every good and perfect gift is from above'*, and that *'we are not our own, but have been bought with a price'*, should motivate us to act wisely in order to increase the Kingdom of Heaven. When we have experienced an increase in the investment that the Master has made in our lives, then we can be assured of His approval. On the day of reckoning, then, we will hear His commendation—*"Well done, good and faithful servant; you have been faithful over a few things, I will make you ruler over many things: enter into the joy of your Lord"*.

For to everyone that has, Jesus concluded, *more shall be given, and he shall have abundance.* In a valuable lesson in spiritual economics, we learn that the one who "has" or "lays hold of" the riches of the kingdom will be given more to the point of "abundance" or overflow". Conversely, *to him that that has not, shall be taken away—even what he has.* If we fail to lay hold of the riches of the kingdom, choosing to accumulate them for ourselves rather than using them to increase the kingdom of Heaven, we stand to lose even the little morsels that we have hoarded.

FEEDING THE HUNGRY

"Then the King will say to those on His right, . . . I was hungry, and you gave Me {something} to eat . . .
Matt 25:34 & 35

It had been a long time since Jenna Harmor had sat in church. Even now she didn't quite know what she was doing here, she just knew that it felt so good to sit once more listening to the words that were spoken by the man behind the pulpit. Memories of her childhood flashed through her mind as she listened to the minister expounding on the account of the guests that had been invited to the wedding feast but had refused to come. In the words she could see the reflection of her life's story. She had been sent to 'church-school' as a child, but had never been challenged on a personal level to do anything more than to 'try to live a good life'. All of her efforts now seemed to be so futile.

Having been unsuccessful in her chosen career, her short marriage had been a disaster from the beginning, and now, as a single mother of two young children, she was still struggling with the concept of unconditional acceptance. It wasn't as if she had never heard the 'gospel story'. Indeed she had heard it repeatedly—but, like the invited guests of whom the preacher was talking, it had never seemed important enough to elicit a response. She had simply ignored the invitation. Now she struggled with the concept that, perhaps, it was too late for her to respond.

"But go into the highways and byways and compel them to come in . . ." That pretty well summed up her feelings this morning. Having wandered so aimlessly on the back roads of life, it seemed that her encounter with Sonya Barnett, last Friday, had been something of a divine appointment. It was the fervency of Sonya's excitement that had compelled Jenna to respond to her invitation. So here she sat this morning, pondering the feeling of anticipation that she felt rising within her. She

needed to talk more deeply with Sonya, and she was almost ashamed of the sense of urgency that made her wish the minister would conclude the sermon.

It was a delicious meal that Sonya had served, but even more satisfying had been the afternoon discussion that had lasted for several hours. As Jenna said "goodnight" to the children and made herself ready for bed, the aching feeling of failure and loneliness oppressed her once more. How she longed for the security of a loving relationship such as she had witnessed in the home of Pastor Phil and Sonya Barnett. What was it that gave them such peace and contentment? As she had listened to their story that afternoon, she found herself longing for the satisfaction that they had said she could experience. She reached for the small New Testament that Sonya had given her, and opened it to the page that held the red silk ribbon. Her eyes fell on the verse that Pastor Phil had hi-lighted in red. *For God so loved the world that He gave His only Son . . .* She knew that she had been touched by that love today, and it felt so good that she longed for more.

For God did not send His Son into the world to condemn the world . . . that was another concept that boggled her mind. She had always felt that God would not accept her because of the mess that she had made of her life. Now it appeared that God did not condemn her, but that He longed for her to be His child. Yes, that was one thing she had always desired—the satisfaction of knowing that she was wanted. She sat in the stillness of her room for some time, and considered the pattern of her past relationships and her desire to be needed.

Phil Barnett closed his bible and glanced with pleasure at the sleeping form of his wife, nestled into the pillow beside him. As she often did, Sonya had fallen into a satisfied slumber as he read aloud from the Word of Life. He whispered a prayer of thanksgiving to God for her love and support, and with a sigh of satisfaction, he leaned over and extinguished the bedside lamp. Then his thoughts turned to the turmoil of his church situation. So many questions swirled in his mind—questions to which he couldn't seem to find the answer. When he couldn't think any longer, he sighed a prayer for increased wisdom, and finally drifted off to sleep.

His slumber was interrupted by the sharp ringing of the bedside telephone. Not wanting Sonya to be aroused, he quickly grabbed the receiver, and mumbled "Hello". The only sound he heard on the other end of the line was a muffled weeping, and a broken voice that hesitantly called his name. Recognizing the voice, he began to speak words of comfort to Jenna Harmor. Assuring her that he did not mind the lateness of the call, he listened patiently to her agonizing confession. Obviously, Jenna was ready to receive the Word of Truth, and Phil was ready to impart it to her.

Sonya was awake now, and Pastor Phil knew that she was praying fervently, as he lead the penitent late-night caller in the sinner's prayer. With a sigh of satisfaction, as he replaced the telephone, he was sure that he heard the sound of a heavenly choir, announcing to all eternity, that another sinner had come home. *She'll come if she's hungry enough*, his words of advice to Sonya reverberated in his mind, *what we need to do is to make sure that there is food on the table when she arrives*. He recalled the nights he had spent in tearful intercession for his flock—could this be the beginning of something new?

Over the next few months it was a joy to watch the young believer open like a flower to the refreshing rain of the Holy Spirit. As the water of the word washed over her weary spirit, Jenna Harmor found healing from the hurt caused by the patterns of rejection and disappointment in her life. Now, it was a blessing to see her, present at the table every week, hungering and thirsting after righteousness, and it was so fulfilling to watch that hunger being satisfied with the Bread of Life. Nothing could have been more rewarding, however, than the day Ian McDuff, the treasurer, handed Phil a sealed envelope that had been dropped into the morning offering plate. It was clearly addressed to "Pastor Phil" and was obviously meant for his eyes only.

Hesitantly, Pastor Phil slit open the envelope, and retrieved a computer-generated "Thank-you" card that displayed a banquet table laden with a sumptuous amount of food. Opening the card, his eyes were drawn to the words printed in an elegant font—*Then shall the king say to those on the right . . . I was hungry and you gave me something to eat*. He felt the emotion rising within him as he read the hand-written sentiment—"Pastor Phil, thank-you for feeding me when I was hungry". The signature read—Jenna Harmor.

Spiritual hunger, like its physical counterpart, has a variety of ways in which it becomes manifest. It may be a casual feeling of necessity for sustenance, or it may be a more severe compelling force. However acute it may be, the result of hunger is a drive to be satisfied. We live in a society in which hunger is regarded as something of a tragedy, and so it is in the physical realm. Certainly, it is emotionally disturbing to view pictures of the less fortunate in third-world countries who must face each day knowing the discomfort of an unsatisfied hunger.

Still, when it comes to experiencing spiritual hunger, Jesus taught that we are actually blessed. Not because God takes pleasure in our discomfort, but rather that He has promised that the 'spiritually hungry' shall be filled or satisfied. As we hunger and thirst after righteousness, we discover a deeper level of God-consciousness, and our lives become more conformed to His image. Note that the object of Jesus teaching in this particular passage of scripture was not simply a matter of self-satisfaction, but rather it was a desire to witness the hunger of others being satisfied. *Love does not seek for it's own fulfillment,* Paul says in I Corinthians 13, *it is more concerned with the satisfaction of others.*

Feeding those who demonstrate a spiritual hunger is not simply a matter of preaching a great Sunday-morning sermon, although that is certainly necessary. While that level of ministry is usually reserved for members of the clergy, Jesus was referring to a much broader ministerial base, which potentially includes every believer. All of us need to know how to break the bread of life to the spiritually hungry. Whether it is a particularly applicable scripture verse, a Spirit-inspired word of wisdom, or a sympathetic ear to a troubled soul, Jesus indicates that our inheritance in the Kingdom of Heaven is assured by our desire to satisfy the hungry people that we meet each day. When we make this act of love a daily priority, we may well be surprised at the number of people to whom we have ministered when we stand before the Judgement Seat. We need to be conscious of the principle that, as Jesus said, *what we do to the very least of these, we do to Him.*

SATISFYING THE THIRSTY

"Then the King will say to those on His right, . . . I was thirsty, and you gave Me something to drink
                                                                Matt 25:34 & 35

Kathy Graham parked the aging Ford Taurus in the designated stall. The underground parking area was a lonely place at 9:30 PM. Wearily, she retrieved the two bags of groceries from the back seat and made her way to the elevator. When she reached the door to her apartment she heard the sound of the ringing telephone. Dropping the groceries, she scrambled to retrieve the key from her purse, and fumbled with the lock. The telephone was still ringing when the lock finally yielded to the key. The call-display window indicated that the caller was her brother, Bob, but, just as she grabbed the receiver, and mumbled "Hello?", the line went dead.

It had been happening with increasing regularity lately. Though they lived in the same city, it used to be months between their visits, but in the past few weeks, their contact had been on a daily basis. How thankful she was, as she considered the spiritual growth that she had witnessed in the lives of her brother and sister-in-law. Every day brought new questions from the spiritually thirsty couple, and she often questioned her adequacy in assuming the role of their spiritual mentor. Now, she pushed the "call-back" button, and waited until she heard Bob's salutation.

"So, you are home," Bob's good-natured banter responded to her salutation. "I was beginning to think that you had moved away without telling anyone!" She knew that he was merely joking with her, but she couldn't help missing the opportunity for a come-back.

"I can't afford to move away", she countered, "who would take care of my kid brother?" They continued to talk at some length before Bob came to the purpose of his initial call. He had been given the opportunity to share his experience at another grief-management seminar that week-end,

69

and wanted to invite her to attend. Her mind was spinning as she hung up the receiver, exulting once more at the reverse of roles that she had witnessed in the past months. Her brother had progressed quickly from the grief-stricken father, to a sympathetic minister of comfort to those who had experienced similar emotional upheavals. How good God had been to the brokenhearted couple.

Still, she wondered once more at the feeling of melancholy that seemed to invade her apartment. Maybe it was just a "stage" that she was going through, but, since that night she had spent ministering to her broken-hearted brother, it seemed that her own spiritual life had been "put on hold". It had been a pleasure to witness the spiritual growth that had occurred in Bob and Sheila's individual lives, as well as their marriage. She turned once more to the solitary apartment, and began to make preparations for another lonely evening. Just before she extinguished the bedside lamp that night, Kathy made a note on the calendar in the "Friday" square to remind her of her promise to Bob.

There was a heaviness that seemed to pervade the spirits of those in attendance tonight, and Bob Graham could well identify with the emotions of the group. Among others whom he did not know he recognized Betty Kimball who had so recently lost her mother in a tragic car accident. A few seats from her sat John and Joyce Freeman whose teenage son had overdosed on drugs two months ago. There were others whom he knew, and some who were strangers to him, but all of them were linked with a common bond. Collectively, they were struggling to come to grips with the grief that seemed, at times, more than they were able to bear. Bob Graham knew the overwhelming sense of loss that the majority of them faced tonight, but he also knew the answer to their release.

The pastor gave the crowd a slight insight into Bob's experience as a word of introduction, Bob prayed fervently that the Holy Spirit would give him the right words to say. As the presentation unfolded, Bob could feel the anointing of the Spirit guiding him. The reflection of the faces in the audience assured him that they were understanding and receiving the truths that God had taught him through his experience. Surveying the ones who had gathered, his eyes fell on the familiar brown hair and pale green eyes of his sister. Bob hadn't noticed her arrival, but a look of recognition passed between them. He realized that Kathy's eyes were moist with emotion as she relived his ordeal with him. She blushed slightly as Bob told the group how valuable it was, in his time of grief, to have someone who would call periodically just to check 'to see how he was doing'.

Then shall the King say, Bob quoted the verse as the conclusion to his seminar, *I was thirsty, and you gave me something to drink.*

Satisfying the thirst, much like the satisfying of hunger, is another one of the basic motivations of the human body. In fact, many times the two concepts are inevitably linked to form a single consideration. Blessed are they that hunger and thirst after righteousness, Jesus commended, for they shall be filled. Still, upon further contemplation, we are able to detect a slight difference between the two concepts. Satisfying the hunger is a process of sustaining and maintaining the growth of the body. Satisfying the thirst aids in the process of digestion of the food we eat, as well as the elimination of the waste products that are unnecessary, and even potentially harmful to the body. In fact, the intake of fluids cleanses not only the digestive tract, but also the circulatory system.

With such a definition in mind, we can better relate to the apostle Paul's analogy of Christ's relationship to the church when he states that *He (Christ) cleanses her (the Church) by the washing of water, with the word.* As we share the water of the word with those who thirst, we aid in cleansing them from the unnecessary waste that they ingest simply because they are in the world, even though they are not of the world. It may seem like an insignificant act at the time, but again Jesus said that *whoever shall give a cup of cold water in My name . . . shall not lose his reward.*

ENTERTAINING STRANGERS

"Then the King will say to those on His right, . . . I was a stranger, and you invited Me in . . .
Matt 25:34 & 35

The old green house at 1125 Fairmont Avenue wasn't much different from any of the other houses that could be found in that neighborhood, but to Jim Daniels it seemed like a bit of heaven. His mind wandered back to the first time that he had been brought to this place . . .

It was almost sixteen years ago, and Jim had been a rebellious teenager, angry at the world, but craving recognition and acceptance. The social worker had advised him that this was only a temporary placement, until a space became available at the group home. "Oh well, so much for 'family stability'!" Jim Daniels grinned cynically at the concept that he had heard so much about, but had never yet experienced. It had been third placement in the last year—and-a-half, so he figured that it may be good for another six or eight months. That appeared to be the limit to people's patience with Jim, who seemed to have an unavoidable propensity toward mischief.

He had been introduced to the Crofton family a few weeks prior. He didn't quite know what to make of their attitude—they were so unlike any home where he had ever been placed before. They seemed almost too 'gushy' for the young Jim Daniels—were these people 'for-real'? There were two kids in the family—Thomas, who was a year older than Jim, and Tracy, who was two years younger. His social worker had indicated that it was for that reason that this family had been chosen as the ideal placement for him.

After thirteen months of living with the Croftons, young Jim Daniels almost dared to believe that he had finally found a family. Hesitantly at first, but then with more familiarity, he found himself referring to the elder Croftons as 'Mom' and 'Dad'. He found that he was under the same privileges and constraints as Thomas and Tracy, as well as enjoying the same recognition and approval. It was still so incomprehensible to Jim.

Adding to his bewilderment was the fact that this was a 'Christian family'. Jim had been taught to be wary of any and all Christians. But with the gentle, consistent love of these people, Jim found himself being drawn into their faith. If this was love, he wanted to know everything about it. The constant exposure to the Gospel through Sunday church services, and the Friday night Youth Group inevitably convinced Jim of his need for a Savior's love. By the time he graduated from high school, Jim knew that he was headed for a career in ministering to Youth in the same manner that he had received so freely.

Over the years, Jim had maintained contact with the Croftons, though his career had required some geographic distance. Two years ago he had grieved with the family over the loss of 'Dad' Crofton, then, last June, Tracy had phoned to tell him that 'Mom' wasn't doing well either. It wasn't too much of a shock, then, to receive another phone call on Monday that 'Mom' had gone home to be with her Lord. With the scenes of the funeral service fresh in his mind, Jim Daniels walked across the street to the house on Fairmont Avenue.

Praying for just the right words of comfort for the grieving brother and sister, Jim hesitantly rang the doorbell. The emotion was still evident in the eyes of both Tracy and Thomas as he embraced them each in turn. They sat for some time, each sharing pleasant memories of the impact that both Mom and Dad had made in their lives. When it was time to take his leave, Jim reached for the plastic bag that he had been carrying.

"I want you to have this in memory of your parents. It's just my way of saying 'thanks' to both of them for the influence they had in my life." Fresh tears of emotion brimmed in both siblings' eyes as Tracy retrieved an elegant, handcrafted plaque from the bag. In bold lettering it declared—*"Then shall the King say . . . I was a stranger and you took me in . . ."*

"Yes," Tracy mused, "those were probably the first words that Mom heard as she entered Glory!"

Be not forgetful to entertain strangers: the Apostle Paul exhorted the Hebrew believers, *for thereby some have entertained angels unawares.* In fact, from the earliest of God's commandments to His people, we find references to the ministry of mercy to strangers. We all remember the first verse that we ever memorized—*For God so loved the world . . .* but so often in our modern world we forget His admonition to share the gospel with every creature. Many, who have been faithful to that commandment will truly be surprised in Heaven to find just how many lives they have touched by a simple act of kindness.

I was a stranger, the King declared, *and you took me in*. It is interesting to note that the words 'took me in' can also be translated to gather, or to join together. The drive for acceptance, the need to be included as 'one of the group' is so acute in some people that, by their actions, they at times become repulsive. The more they strive to be accepted, the more they find themselves 'excluded from the group'. For those who are not sensitive to such actions, these people appear to be deserving of their fate. Jesus, however, surrounded himself with those who were unacceptable to society. Who else would have chosen a 'tax-collector' as part of His ministry team, and who would have allowed a 'prostitute' to anoint Him for His burial?

But the trouble with a lot of Christians is that they are so gullible—they simply accept anybody and everybody. Doesn't the Bible say that we are to be "wise as serpents? . . ." Many of us have heard the argument countless times. The implication being that, in accepting the sinner, we become a partner to his sins. Such was not the case in Jesus' ministry. By responding to the invitation to dinner at Simon's house, Jesus was clearly not capitulating to the pharisaical mindset. That became quite clear in His firm rebuke to the smug host. Nor was He condoning the lifestyle of the woman who had come to minister to Him. Clearly, Jesus cut to the heart of the matter with His declaration—*Your sins have been forgiven*! If we can glean any example from Jesus style of ministry, it would be that, in His sight, there is an acute distinction between the sin and the sinner. God hates all sin, but He loves all sinners. That is a principle that we would do well to remember as we seek to fulfill the ministry that he has committed to us.

Because of the message of love and hope with which we have been entrusted, we will often find some of the most undesirable of characters being drawn to us. Rather than ignoring them, or even turning away from them, Jesus taught that we should provide them with the measure of acceptance that they so desperately crave. A simple act of including them in our circle of fellowship will so often give them the strength that they need to abandon their undesirable actions. In a sobering application of such a principle, Jesus reminds us that, ultimately, in so ministering to the needs of others, we minister to Him.

CLOTHING THE NAKED

Then the King will say to those on His right . . . I was naked and you clothed me . . .
                                                    Matt 25:34 & 35

Old age did not come gracefully to Alice Cheevers. Alice had always been one to be involved, especially when it came to serving the family of God. There was a time when she had thought nothing of attending four church functions in a week, and she still had time for her extended family. Now, it seemed to be a chore to get dressed for Sunday Morning church, to be ready for her nephew Carl as he came to take her to fellowship with the saints. Sometimes she wondered if she hadn't been 'set on the shelf' spiritually, when she considered the joyous experiences that she witnessed in the lives of younger believers in her sphere of influence.

"Now Alice," she chided herself, "we haven't arranged for the caterers for any pity party". She let her mind focus on the wonders that God had worked in her family's life in the past twenty years. 'Twenty years' had once sounded synonymous to eternity, yet today it seemed like yesterday. Truly, life had been all she had ever hoped for—and a lot more. Her teaching career had allowed her to impact so many young lives, and she, in turn, had learned so much from each of her students. Her moment of reflection was broken by the carillon sound of the chimes at the front door.

Her nephew, Carl, stood at the door with that enigmatic grin as she opened to answer his salutation. "Ready to go?" he queried as Alice reached for her coat. Carl held her coat as she slipped it on, and then held the door for her as she slipped outside into the crisp morning air. For all he had suffered in his formative years, Alice never ceased to be amazed at the gentle manner of the young man that escorted her to his waiting car. She remembered the emotional pain that she had often witnessed in his eyes as, at a tender age he had dealt with the disappointment of a broken home, and a workaholic father. She recalled the resolve of Carl, the teenager who was determined to fulfill the expectations of his peers as well as his parents. Scenes of his Graduation Day played on the screen of her memory as they pulled into the church parking lot. Still, the most important memory of all had to be the exultant look on twenty year-old Carl's face when he told her of his decision to follow Christ. For all of his quiet, unassuming personality, Carl Cheevers was truly a testimony to the ever-abundant grace of God.

The morning was a refreshing time of praise and worship, including a generous portion of spiritual sustenance as the entire congregation feasted on the Word of God. All too soon, it seemed, the morning had ended and, once more, Carl walked his Aunt Alice to the waiting Ford Escort in the church parking lot. "Can I buy you lunch?" Carl suggested, as he maneuvered the car into the noon hour traffic. The prospect of another lonely Sunday afternoon caused Alice to answer in the affirmative. Carl grinned knowingly as he pulled into the parking lot of the Perkins Restaurant on the corner of Century and Marlboro.

They were slightly ahead of the usual Sunday lunch-time crowd, so Carl was able to choose a booth near the picture window overlooking the scenic Rainbow Park. Alice smiled unconsciously, as she recalled the many hours she had spent with Carl in his adolescent years in the safe confines of the picturesque Park. Without much delay, the waitress came to take their order, then they were left in the solitude of each others company, awaiting the delivery of their lunch-time orders.

Carl talked animatedly about his plans for university in the fall where he would be pursuing a career as a high-school physical education instructor. Once again, Alice's heart warmed as she remembered the drive that had always consumed Carl whenever he had been involved in academic sports. She recalled the many times that Carl had invited, no—almost pleaded with her to attend his softball games when his father's work schedule had prevented his parent's attendance.

The conversation stalled while they feasted on the food that was set before them. Finally, it was Carl that pursued the dialogue once more. "Is everything alright, Aunt Alice?" Carl offered hesitantly. Again, Alice was impressed with her nephew's depth of perception. She searched momentarily for the words to explain her feelings to the serious young man addressing her so knowingly. Aware of her transparency before him, Alice began to share her 'mid-life blues' with Carl. He listened to her deepest thoughts politely, occasionally asking for clarification of some points. When she was finished, he continued to observe her in silence. She knew that he was collecting his thoughts, and she felt a stab of remorse at having unloaded her emotions onto the young man. Were those tears in his eyes?

At last, when he spoke, Carl's voice was slightly husky with emotion. *"I was naked, and you clothed me,"* he began, as Alice mentally scrambled to comprehend the connection between such a statement and their current conversation. Vaguely, she recalled changing the infant Carl's diaper a few times, often filling in as a surrogate mother during his adolescent and teenage years. Once more, Carl picked up on her inability to grasp the significance of such a statement. "You were the only 'Mother' I ever really knew," he explained, "and for that I am truly thankful. When I needed encouragement, you were there, when I needed direction, I knew that I could come to you. When Mom and Dad were too busy to come and watch our Little League championship game, I remember you sitting in the third row of the stands, cheering us on. When I felt guilty over what happened to Mom and Dad's relationship, you were the one who helped me to understand that it wasn't my fault." With each memory, Alice felt her own emotions on the rise.

Reaching for her hand across the table, Carl looked solemnly into her eyes. "Dear Aunt Alice," he concluded, "don't ever let the enemy convince you that God would ever 'set you on the shelf'. You're much too valuable in the Kingdom of Heaven for Him to allow that to happen." In the moment of silent communion that followed, the waitress set their orders on the table and left them once again in their solitude. "Now, eat your lunch . . ." he admonished in a tone of voice which she recognized as an echo of her own motherly instruction to the adolescent Carl. Once again he grasped her hand, as he unashamedly offered a prayer of thanksgiving for the food on the table before them.

If there is one principle to which we can all agree, it would be that 'life isn't always a bed of roses'. Whether we can relate to it in our own lives, or in the lives of those we love, we can recall times that have left wounds and scars that only the love of God will ever be able to heal. When Jesus talked of being 'naked', people throughout the ages can relate to such an experience as the ultimate form of humiliation. It is one thing to be mildly embarrassed by the people or circumstances to which we are exposed, but humiliation is an experience that breaks the spirit of the victim. People who have been humiliated in their lives will carry a stigma of shame to which others may find it hard to relate. Because of the emotional walls that they build around themselves in order to prevent a recurrence of the shameful experience, they may appear to those around them to be entirely unapproachable. In fact, their defense systems may be so far advanced that they appear to be quite 'normal', until some experiential stimulus ignites the catastrophic explosion that has been so well hidden for such a long time. To these people, Jesus said, we can have a special ministry of 'clothing them' or covering their shame.

It may involve something as simple as lending a sympathetic ear to their hurts and disappointments, or it may mean directing them to a source of more intense spiritual counseling. Whatever action we take, it should be accompanied by much prayer and unconditional love on our part.

Unfortunately, there are too many times when a well-meaning, but entirely misled brother or sister in Christ, attempts to deal with the situation in their own strength and according to their own limited knowledge. Such action is often more devastating to the wounded one than the original incident. We need to remember that Paul said—Love is patient, and love is kind. Keeping in mind such principles will give us the compassion that we see in Jesus' ministry to those that needed his touch.

As part of His suffering prior to His crucifixion, we find that Jesus was stripped of His robes, and suffered the humiliation of mockery at the hands of the Roman soldiers. It may provide some consolation to the modern-day sufferer that our Lord knows and understands the effects of humiliation at the hands of human nature.

We may not always have a sound theological answer to the hurts and disappointments of others; all we need to do is *'cover their nakedness'*. In so doing, we make sure that they feel safe and comfortable in our company, and they will know that we do not regard their shame as something that is repulsive to us.

VISITING THE SICK

Then the King will say to those on His right . . . I was sick and you visited me . . .

Matt 25:34 & 35

Perhaps it was a matter of personal conjecture, but, to the perceptive mind of Keith Proctor, it appeared that, lately, a spirit of discouragement had surrounded George Barker. For a moment, Keith found his thoughts wandering from the words that Pastor Harvey Bernatti was speaking in exhortation to the flock. George had often appeared to be preoccupied lately, and the spiritual fervor, which had so long been his trademark, seemed to have waned. Keith made a mental note to discuss the matter with his wife, June, before they retired tonight.

"For I was sick, and you visited me" . . . the voice of Pastor Harvey, reading his text from Matthew's Gospel, drew Keith back to the reality of the present. He felt a quickening in his spirit as the Pastor expounded on the necessity for the believers to invest time and effort in the lives of those who are physically, as well as spiritually weak. Had it not been for the patient, faithful ministry of people like George Barker and Pastor Harvey, Keith shuddered to think of where his marriage would be today. The thought caused his right hand to tighten around June's shoulder as he sat with his arm comfortably draped around her on the back of the pew. June stirred slightly at his touch, and nestled closer in his embrace as they continued to drink-in the refreshing water of the word.

Keith guided the automobile into the parking lot at the Three-D Restaurant on Regent Avenue, wondering whom they would meet today. It was customary for a few members of the congregation to take pleasure in a leisurely Sunday lunch—enjoying each other's fellowship, and discussing the needs of the Body of Christ.

"It looks like George is here anyway," June's excited voice caused Keith to follow her gaze until he recognized the aging Ford Escort parked not far from the front entrance. Keith breathed a silent prayer for wisdom as he parked the car in the adjacent parking stall. When they entered the front door, Keith met George's gaze and nodded in silent recognition. He followed a few paces behind June as she excitedly made her way to join George at his table.

"Where's everyone else?" June's exuberance was evident as she approached George at the table.

Keith sensed uneasiness in George's demeanor as he hesitantly replied—"I guess it's just the two of you and me today!" It almost seemed to be a relief to George to realize that their fellowship would be restricted to the three of them. The waitress brought their orders and they bowed for a moment of thanksgiving before hungrily attacking what was placed before them.

"How much do you guys know about Alzheimer's Disease?" George blurted out after finishing his second cup of coffee. June's eyes grew wide, and Keith almost choked on the mouthful of coffee that he had just taken. It was a shocking turn to the otherwise silent communion and their minds swirled as they tried to grasp the significance of George's question.

Was he saying . . . ? Keith's mind refused to complete the question. He glanced quickly at June, and, seeing that her eyes glistened with tears, knew that she had come to the same conclusion. "Not much . . ." he mumbled, "why do you ask?"

George detected the panic in their expressions, and was instantly sorry for the abruptness of the question. "Don't worry, it's not for myself!" he assured them, "I'm a little young to be in any danger of that!" Both June and Keith breathed sighs of relief, and then chuckled as the realization of their hasty conclusions permeated their consciousness. George went on to explain the recent diagnosis reached with regards to his aging mother. They were aware of the special relationship that existed between George and his mother. Having suffered the loss of her husband a few years after their marriage, George's mother had never remarried, and had raised her son on her own efforts.

They listened painfully as George related the experiences of witnessing his mother's progression through the various stages of the debilitating disease. Now, it seemed that the only solution offered by the 'experts' was to confine his mother to a personal care home where she could receive 24-hour personal attention. He explained the feelings of guilt over having to leave his mother in the care of strangers, but the viability of any other options was almost non-existent.

Trying to offer the much-needed support to the grieving brother, June found herself assuring George that 'they understood his grief', and that 'if he ever needed to talk, just to give them a call'. Even to June's mind, the statement almost seemed 'trite'.

"Thank-you", George responded, clearly struggling with his emotions, "you don't know how much that means to me."

Two years had passed since George had shared his trepidation and fears with the Proctors. There had been times when the grief in George's eyes was almost too painful to witness. Still, they felt the obligation to visit the aging Mrs. Barker at least once every week. The time spent during each visit, just trying to remind her who they were often caused June to weep openly in sympathy for the family's pain. The prayers of the saints had, over time, shifted from *"Let this cup pass . . ."* to *"nevertheless, not our will but Thine be done . . ."*

It shouldn't have been such a shock, June puzzled, when Pastor Harvey had called that morning to inform them of Mrs. Barker's passing. She wondered, almost remorseful, at the sense of relief that she felt as she had dialed Keith's office number to pass on the dreaded, but inevitable news. As they sat in the solemnity of the memorial service now, wondering if there was anything more they could have done, June's eye caught the significance of the inscription on the program sheet. Along with a note of gratitude to the Body for their practical and emotional support was the declaration: *"Then shall the King say . . . I was sick, and you visited me . . ."*

Nobody ever said that the Christian life would be easy, in fact, for the most part, many would agree that in their experience it has been 'anything but'. One of the most dreaded parts of that experience for many in the Kingdom includes the ministry of visiting the sick, or weak. Many would concur that, when we speak of sickness, it is not necessarily the physical body that is indicated. Certainly, those with any amount of experience in life can identify times when they have also witnessed, if not experienced, spiritual and emotional sickness.

Whatever category of "weakness" may confront us, it is common to feel a sense of repulsion at the situation. Many can relate to the uneasiness that one experiences in the presence of such a scenario. After all, if we are really Jesus' disciples, shouldn't we be able to 'heal the sick' as He said we would be able to? We may even be faced with the question of who is lacking faith—is it the victim, or does the deficiency lie in our own lives? Or, possibly we are struggling with the question that faced the disciples of Jesus as they were confronted with the blind man—*'Lord, who sinned, this man, or his parents?'* Because of the ramifications of the possible answers to such soul-searching questions, many disciples opt for the solution of avoidance. 'Out of sight, out of mind' the old proverb dictates, if we can avoid witnessing the problem, we won't have to think on it. Additionally, the enemy won't have any basis for his condemnation as to the level of our faith.

We would do well to remind ourselves in such situations that the Master in Jesus parable didn't commend the faithful on the basis of 'I was sick, and you ministered complete healing to me.' Rather, the recognition was based merely on the fact that the dedicated servants were available to periodically 'look in on' or 'check on the welfare of' the afflicted. Many who have for themselves, or for close friends or relatives, suffered the indignity of any prolonged, debilitating weakness can attest to the reticence of even the most well-meaning saints to maintain a schedule of consistent visitation. For the most part, such duties are usually relegated to the pastor of the flock. After all, that's what he is getting paid for, isn't it? When, at the end of time, the Master commends the faithful with the benediction—*I was sick and you visited Me* . . . I am sure that He will be addressing more than ordained members of the clergy. Similarly, when the pronouncement is made to the negligent, no one will be able to use the excuse—but Lord, I thought that was the pastor's job!

Undoubtedly, it will necessitate moving out of our comfort zone in order for us to effect this portion of our ministry. More importantly, it will require an investment of our time and effort, but no one can deny that Jesus indicated that such an investment would yield valuable eternal returns.

MINISTERING IN PRISON

Then the King will say to those on His right . . . I was in prison, and you came to me . . .
                                            Matt 25:34 & 35

Today was April 18th, and Marcie Baldwin had that 'melancholy feeling' once more. It happened every year at this time, although, with the passing of the seasons, the pain was not as acute as it once had been. Eighteen April 18ths had come and gone, and still, Marcie wondered. She wondered what had ever become of Billy Wheeler. Today would be his twenty-first birthday. Where was he now? What was he doing? He probably would have graduated from high school a few years ago, maybe he had gone to college? Perhaps he was pursuing a career by now? One hundred and one questions had gone through her mind countless times, and still she had no answers. Lost in her thoughts, she was drawn back to reality when she felt a pair of arms gently surround her, and a light kiss on the back of her neck. She turned and allowed herself to melt into the embrace of her husband, Ed Baldwin. Ed was the only one who knew what today meant to her, and she thanked God for his understanding and support.

Eighteen years ago, after a short, turbulent relationship with Billy's father, the prospect of raising a child on her own efforts had seemed impossible—not only to herself, but also in the judgment of the social services case worker. Confused and alone, and 'for the sake of the child', heeding the counsel of the caseworker, she had placed Billy on the list for adoption. Certain family members and 'friends' had been openly critical of her actions, but, for the most part, her newly found church-family had given her the love and support that she so desperately needed. She recalled her struggles with regret over the foolishness of her youth, and the blatant condemnation of some of the more 'mature' members of the Body of Christ. She had found some release in the truth that God no longer remembered the sins of her youth—that they had been cast into the sea of His forgetfulness—but still she wondered . . .

Marcie became aware of the fact that Ed still had his arms around her, but now he was whispering in her ear. As she listened, she realized that he was praying that God would give her strength, that He would grant the 'desires of her heart', and that He would 'cause all things to work together for good, because of Marcie's love for Him'. When Ed's voice fell silent, they spent a few moments just drinking-in the Father's love and comfort.

The ringing of the telephone intruded on their quiet time, and Marcie felt Ed's embrace tighten in an unspoken admonition to 'let it ring'. For a moment she considered that line of action, but her curiosity got the better of her, and she squirmed free of his embrace. After a short dash across the living-room, she snatched the telephone receiver from the cradle, and managed a breathless "Hello?"

"Hello," a professional-sounding female voice greeted her, "is this Marcella Baldwin?"

Having confirmed her identity, the woman proceeded to introduce herself as Joan Montgomery, a case worker with the Department of Social Services. She went on to explain that the Department had recently received an inquiry from a young man whose birth-name was William Wheeler, and was interested in making contact with his natural mother. Following through various government records, they had traced her to this telephone number, and needed to confirm that such a meeting would be agreeable to her. Joan Montgomery assured Marcie that none of the information acquired in the process of contacting her would be passed on to the young man without her express permission.

Marcie was stunned, and remained speechless for several moments. When she finally recovered her voice, she vaguely remembered giving her assent to the procedure. Joan assured her that she would be in contact with her to arrange the details of such an encounter. In a daze she hung up the telephone and turned to face Ed once more. "Are you alright?" Ed queried as he again enveloped her in a loving embrace. Marcie burst into uncontrollable sobbing. For the next several minutes, between floods of emotion, Ed was able to piece together the general purpose of the phone call.

When the initial shock of the telephone call subsided, Marcie found herself questioning the wisdom of her initial response. Still, she couldn't deny the emotional ache that she had so often experienced. Were her wildest dreams now going to become a reality? Her spirit cried out to God for His wisdom and the emotional strength that she would need to face the young man. What would he think of her? How should she respond to him? Her mind was racing a mile a minute, flooded with one thousand and one questions. Into her turmoil the quiet voice of the Holy Spirit seemed to echo the words that Ed had used in his prayer—*And we know that all things work together for good* . . .

Tuesday morning dawned just the same as any other day, but Marcie felt a strange sense of foreboding as she opened her eyes. With her awakening came the awareness that 'this was the day'! She became conscious that the excitement and anticipation had kept her awake until after 1:00 am this morning. She would have to meet Joan Montgomery at her office at 10:00 am. Ed was awakening beside her now, and feeling her tension, he gently took her hand and continued to speak soothing words of comfort to her. Vaguely, Marcie remembered arising and preparing for the day. The excitement prevented her from having too much for breakfast—a bran muffin and a cup of coffee was all that her stomach could handle.

A young man sat in the chair next to the coffee table as Marcie entered Joan Montgomery's office. His hair fell, unkempt, around his shoulders. He wore faded blue jeans, and a white fleece sweater that unashamedly proclaimed to the world in red lettering—*Jesus—He's the real thing!* His brown eyes were shining as he stood to acknowledge her entry. "B-Billy?" Marcie heard herself stammer as she recognized her own facial features reflected in the image of her son.

"Hello Mom," he returned with ease, as he stepped forward to encircle her lightly with his arms in a short, but heartfelt embrace. It wasn't the way she had rehearsed it in her mind, but in that moment Marcie realized that it was everything she had ever dreamed. This was her son—healthy, personable, and obviously *'not ashamed of the gospel of Christ'*. Once more the emotional floodgates burst as she felt her son's embrace tighten around her shoulders. Then came the words that she had so often longed to hear, but had resigned herself to the fact that such a pleasure would never be hers. "I love you, Mom," she heard him whisper unashamedly, as she became aware that he, too, was overcome with the emotion of the moment.

"I'll leave you two to get acquainted," Joan Montgomery advised as she exited the room, feeling a wonderful release that the encounter had gone so smoothly.

The next week was, what Marcie thought must have been, just a taste of what Heaven would be like. As the drama unfolded, Marcie learned that at the age of seven years, a family with the name Cantrell had adopted Billy, and raised him in a Christian environment. Since his high-school graduation, he had pursued a career in education, and had recently started working with a youth organization that ministered to troubled teens. Everyday, Mother and Son were amazed at the 'unsearchable ways' of their Heavenly Father in directing their lives to this moment of satisfaction.

Marcie sat on the sofa with her Bible open on her lap. Tears of joy once more washed her cheeks as she thought on the meaning of the words she had just read. *"I was in prison, and you came to Me . . ."*

From where he sat beside her, she felt Billy's incredulous look, as he stammered—"Prison.?" Why would those words cause such an emotional response in his mother?

"Yes, Billy," she stammered, "I was in prison. High walls of remorse, steel bars of bitterness, and a lifetime of hopes and dreams locked securely behind doors of disappointment. But then you came with God's love and your forgiveness . . .".

Once again, Son took Mother into his comforting embrace as he repeated those words that had brought so much healing to Marcie's spirit in the past few weeks. "I love you, Mom!" That was all she had ever wanted to hear.

It is one of those generally-accepted principles of the Gospel that Jesus came to 'set the prisoner free'. And if we have done any amount of spiritual contemplation, we have probably conceded that the concept is not limited to those who are physically incarcerated. In fact, more often than not in the Christian experience, the 'prisons' are more of a spiritual nature. Due to a variety of circumstances, many people whom we meet will find themselves in confinement to certain feelings or situations. Consider the man who refuses to relate to people of certain ethnic origins because he once had an uncle who was abused by someone of that nationality. Or you may have heard of the mother who dreads sending her son to summer camp because she heard that last year another child developed a serious illness while at that camp. Perhaps you have met the daughter of divorced parents who will not allow herself to develop any serious relationship with a man—in case her life turns out to be the same disaster that caused her parents so much heartache. With a little imagination one can insert their own experience into the applicable scenario.

Whatever the stimulus might be, we can detect 'prisons' of fear, prejudice, bitterness—the list is almost endless. Just as surely as physical walls confine the prisoner, so these feelings and personality traits restrict seemingly 'normal' people. Giving in to the lies of the Enemy, they miss out on some of the greatest blessings which God has to offer. Ministering to such people is, at the best of times, a difficult calling, but we cannot deny that it is a vital part of the work of the believer.

Note that the commendation of the King seems to be extended to those who made a distinct effort to reach out to the ones in prison. Too often we take the judgmental attitude of those who say—you made the bed, now you lie in it. Or, possibly we simply adopt a detached view of the situation that rationalizes—it's not my problem. We need to understand that, for the most part, those in prison are unable to effect their own release. That is why this aspect of the ministry is so very crucial.

Perhaps it is a matter of the author's conjecture, but, as I reflected on this passage, I was impressed by the fact that the commendation by the King goes only as far as—*I was in prison, and you visited me.* One may be tempted at that point to view the ministry as incomplete. Should we not have effected total deliverance for the incarcerated one? Didn't Jesus 'come to set the captives free'? I wonder if sometimes, in our exuberance, we try to take too much upon ourselves, endeavoring to do things that only Jesus can do through the power of the Holy Spirit. The form of ministry in this situation, that garnered the approval of the King was the act of simply 'visiting' or 'coming to' the one who had been imprisoned.

Indeed, it may seem that our efforts are futile, and our ministry is ineffective when we see no change in the spiritual situation of those to whom we minister. In those times, it is comforting to remember that our duty is, primarily, to remain available to those in prison, not leaving them to suffer their tribulations alone. Regardless of our apparent success rate, it would still be more spiritually rewarding to reach out and have our efforts rejected by the blind prisoner, than to incur the Master's rebuke—*"I was in prison and you did not come to me . . ."* It may be a simple 'How are you really doing?' over a cup of coffee at the local restaurant, or a phone-call to say 'I was thinking about you today . . .' No matter how insignificant the gesture may seem to be, Jesus said that it would reap rewards that will follow us into eternity.

LESSONS FROM THE PLAYGROUND

"Truly I say to you, unless you are converted and become like children, you will not enter the kingdom of heaven.
                                                                Matt 18:3

"Mom, come quick! Something's wrong with Tabby!" The panicked voice of her eight-year old son drew Mary Sidney from her study time. It wasn't the first time that she had been interrupted this evening, and Mary wondered, with a slight irritation, what the crisis was all about this time. She considered delaying giving her attention to the latest 'cat-astrophe', but Donny's voice was nearing terror proportions as he continued to summon her. She hurried down the stairs leading to the basement where Donny was wailing over the plight of his pet feline. Tabby lay motionless in the box beside the furnace, and it was apparent that Donny had been trying to rouse her for some time. Suddenly, Mary also developed a sense of dread at the stark possibilities of the situation. Tabby was, after all, a part of the family, and if they were to lose her, Mary dreaded to think of how she would deal with the grief of two adolescent children.

"What's wrong with her, Mom?" Donny continued to ask the question to which Mary had no answer. "Should we pray for her?" Mary was stunned at the question; it was a line of action that would never have occurred to her. Does one pray for a dying cat—or was that just a wee bit childish? Donny sensed her hesitation, so in his desperation he decided to take the situation into his own hands. In all his innocence he placed his trembling hand on Tabby's head, as he had seen the pastor do at church, and began to pray fervently. "Dear Jesus," he stammered, "please heal Tabby, please don't let her die!" Again, Mary shuddered, wondering how she would explain to Donny, if the cat remained motionless. She found herself praying for wisdom as to how to explain to an innocent child the doctrine of 'divine appointment'.

Then, as Donny repeated his heart-wrenching petition for the third time, he suddenly gave a squeal of delight. Mary watched in amazement as the cat stirred, blinked twice, and began to wash a bit of leftover ice cream from Donny's hand. "See Mom?" Donny exulted, "it works!" Feeling slightly rueful for her own lack of faith, Mary turned to her task of preparing supper for the family. She couldn't think of a logical explanation for the preceding moments, but she silently sang a song of praise to God for his love and mercy to an eight year-old child.

"Guess what, Julie?" Donny announced to his older sister, as she shut the door, "Tabby got r-res-resurr." he stumbled over the word, looking to his mother for assistance.

"Resurrected!" Mary supplied the word that escaped his memory.

At eleven years of age, Julie was older and much wiser. "Yeah, right!" she responded with open skepticism to her brother's exuberance. She looked to her mother, expecting that her brother would hear a word of correction for embellishing the truth, but nothing was forthcoming. "Is that right Mom?" she asked, in obvious disbelief.

"Well," Mary struggled for the right words, "I know that Tabby wasn't doing very well at all, but when Billy prayed for her, she came around pretty quickly". Julie offered no further argument as she followed her mother into the kitchen to help prepare for supper.

"Can I spend Friday night at Janet's house?" Julie suggested as they loaded the dishwasher with the dishes from supper. Mary was startled by the question. Just last month, she had spent several hours trying to console Julie, after it became apparent that Janet had spread some nasty rumors about Julie to the other children in her classroom. "Don't worry," Julie continued as if to calm her mother's unspoken fears, "her parents will be home."

"But, last month Janet was being so mean to you at school," Mary was surprised that Julie would even consider accepting the invitation.

"That was before Mrs. Wilson told us about forgiving what other people do to us, so that God will forgive us too!" Julie explained in her purest adolescent wisdom. Laura Wilson certainly had a way of making an impact on young lives, Mary mused silently, as she recovered from the unintended rebuke from her daughter.

"Friday night is fine with me," Mary countered, much to Julie's delight. "Tell Janet to have her Mom call me to make the arrangements."

With the children tucked safely into bed, Mary curled up in her recliner chair with a soothing cup of tea in one hand, and her Bible in the other. As usual, she took a few moments just to reflect on the events of the day.

Verily I say unto you, she read from the eighteenth chapter of Mathew's Gospel, *Except you be converted, and become as little children, you shall not enter into the kingdom of heaven. And whosoever therefore shall humble himself as this little child, the same is greatest in the kingdom of heaven.* She still hadn't quite absorbed the wonder of Donny's prayer for his cat, *But Lord,* she prayed, *help me to have that child-like faith to trust You for what others would deem impossible.* She remembered Julie's request and her ability to so quickly overlook the former wounds that had been inflicted by her closest 'friend'. *And Lord,* she continued, *help me to have the memory of a child when I have to deal with those who offend me. And thank-you so much, Lord for the little children you have given me to teach me so many valuable lessons about You . . .*

Wherever Jesus went, it seemed that He was always surrounded by a flock of children. Much to the consternation, and occasional irritation of His disciples, the little children seemed to usurp the most of Jesus' time and attention. More than once, Jesus had to admonish his followers regarding the importance of the children within the Kingdom of Heaven. The primary requirement for entrance into the kingdom, Jesus was quick to point out, is to become as little children. The concept may be somewhat unnerving to the adult mentality, but when we consider it, we become impressed with the wisdom of such a statement. We remember the innocence of the child's mind, the ability to view every aspect of life with an undefiled wonder. Without the barriers of logic or fear, it is easy to explain to a child the plan of salvation, and the concept of God's everlasting love. Unless we develop that child-like ability to believe God's word as the ultimate truth, Jesus said we will never really enter into the Kingdom of Heaven.

In order to achieve the goal of becoming as little children, Jesus said, we need to humble ourselves. Literally, the word means 'to bring down to a lower plain'. For the most part, to a child, adults are the source of all wisdom. If they ever lack the ability to reason things for themselves, it is logical for a child to seek an explanation from someone who is older and more experienced. As we grow to adulthood, we are taught to 'think for ourselves', and, to a great extent, we lose the ability to seek the counsel of others. Any new concept is met with a measure of skepticism, and a need to reason it out for ourselves. This is why it is much easier to lead a child into a salvation experience than it is to bring an adult into the kingdom of heaven. The adult mind will need to develop the simplicity of a child in order to grasp the principles of the Kingdom of Heaven.

There are so many valuable lessons to be learned from observing the actions and responses of a child. It is little wonder that Jesus encourages us to become like children in order to become great—that is 'large' or 'strong'—in the Kingdom of Heaven.

BAGGAGE HANDLERS ANONYMOUS

And again I say unto you, It is easier for a camel to go through the eye of a needle, than for a rich man to enter into the kingdom of God.

Matt: 19:24

Dwayne Turcotte sat in the third pew on the left-hand side of the sanctuary, listening to Reverend Frank Hansen expound on the 'Principles of the Kingdom' from the nineteenth chapter of Mathew's Gospel. If the scripture was any indication of heaven's entrance exam, Dwayne was thankful that he wasn't rich. The modest, three bedroom bungalow on Spencer Drive that was home to himself and his lovely wife, Donna, was adequate, but certainly couldn't be classified as a 'mansion'. The Ford Mustang they had driven to church this morning was 'sporty', but it wasn't a Cadillac. Their bank account didn't often fall below the $1000 level, but, certainly no one could rightfully accuse the Turcotte's of being 'rich'.

In his reflection, Dwayne realized that his mind had drifted from Frank Hansen's exhortation, but now he became aware of hearing something about a 'camel passing through the eye of the needle'. The concept was so bizarre that Dwayne soon found his mind drifting once again to other, more relevant matters. He must not forget the appointment with Bill Fraser at the bank on Tuesday to review the financing proposal for the expansion of his computer store . . .

But the first shall be last, and the last, first . . . again his attention returned to the words of the pastor. "How can that be fair?" Dwayne questioned in his mind, "for all the effort I've expended to be on top of the computer retailing business, in God's books I might still be in last place?" So much of the Bible was so hard to understand. He was relieved when the pianist returned to the piano and the congregation began to sing the final hymn. But again, the words puzzled him, as the congregation sang about how they'd rather have Jesus than silver or gold . . . A nice concept, Dwayne thought, but he wondered how many people really meant what they were singing about.

"I built this business from nothing!" Dwayne thundered, "and I don't need any punk kid telling me how to run it!" Lance Turcotte had graduated from university with a degree in Business Administration, and Dwayne felt that Lance was always trying to tell his uncle how to run the business. There were times when Dwayne felt intimidated by his young partner, but Lance was, at best, a junior partner, after all. Admittedly, his nephew's advanced education was impressive, compared to his own Grade 12 schooling, but Dwayne certainly had reason to be satisfied with his accomplishments in life. When he was Lance's age, Dwayne had been employed as a stock-boy with a major retail store. Now, he had his own business, and was well versed in the latest technological advances in the computer industry. Nephew Lance simply shrugged in acquiescence to his uncle's tirade, and returned to his preparation of the operating budget that was to be part of the presentation to Bill Fraser tomorrow.

"I'm sorry, Dwayne," Bill Fraser could feel the disappointment settle on his client, "but the application for funding the expansion program has been rejected." This next step in the development of his business was all that Dwayne had thought about for the past number of months. Now, it seemed that his dreams lay shattered on the big oak desk of Bill Fraser. He could tell that any argument would be pointless as Bill explained the bank's reasoning in the face of the sliding economy, coupled with Dwayne's personal lack of any formal business education. The situation presented too much of a risk in the assessment of the Business Development Loans Manager, and Bill was forced to comply with his superior.

Dwayne's mind was reeling as he entered the street. How could something that seemed to be so simple suddenly turn out so wrong? "For all the effort I've expended to be on top of the computer retailing business, in God's books I might still be in last place?" The question raised by Frank Hansen's sermon now echoed in his mind. And what was that about being easier for a camel to go through the eye of a needle, than for a rich man to enter the Kingdom of Heaven? Surely God didn't view him in that light—did He?

When Dwayne arrived back at the storefront, the only one to greet him was Hannah, the cashier. Without questioning, Hannah advised him that Lance had left early, citing a previously arranged appointment—of which Dwayne had no recollection. *"Playing 'hooky' again on company time"* Dwayne thought bitterly, as he began formulating the pep talk he would give the youngster at their next meeting. The balance of the afternoon passed fairly smoothly, although Dwayne felt a pang of resentment every time he thought of his conference with Bill Fraser. He was oblivious to the return of nephew Lance, until the young man stood hesitantly in front of his desk.

"Uncle Dwayne," Lance began hesitantly, "I've been doing a lot of thinking lately . . ." As the conversation unfolded, Lance began to explain to his uncle about what he termed "the call of God on his life". The plan was to leave the business next fall, in order to pursue a career in full-time ministry. Once again, Dwayne's emotions went into a tailspin. Having no child of his own, Dwayne had always envisioned Lance as a surrogate son to whom he could leave the business upon his retirement. The whole idea was so preposterous—why would Lance 'throw away' a good education and a promising career in order to follow some whim? It made no sense, but the more the young man talked, the more determined he became to answer the 'call of God'.

"Life isn't about financial security, or social status, Uncle Dwayne," Lance stated so matter-of-factly, "it's about being obedient to what the Lord wants me to do." It seemed that hours passed while Lance cited arguments involving 'seeking first the kingdom of God and His righteousness', and it being 'easier for a camel to go through the eye of the needle, than for a rich man to enter the kingdom of heaven'. Dwayne wondered where he had heard those statements before? It was all so frustratingly familiar, but Dwayne was still lost in the translation. How could he begin to understand such spiritual concepts when it seemed that God was pulling the rug out from under his life? First it was Bill Fraser's denial of financing, now his nephew was 'thumbing his nose' at everything he had worked so hard to achieve in his lifetime.

"So what's with this 'camel-and-the-eye-of-the-needle'?" Dwayne demanded in exasperation. His impudence soon turned to fascination as Lance explained the concepts of getting rid of all the spiritual baggage in one's life before he could really enjoy all of God's goodness. The more the young man talked, the more it became clear to Dwayne that his own 'baggage' included not only the valuable business that he had developed, but it also involved his pride in his achievements, as well as his fear of failure. By the time the conversation was concluded, Dwayne enjoyed a wonderful sense of release from the burdens with which he had struggled for a lifetime.

The parable that Jesus told regarding the camel and the eye-of-the-needle is probably one of the most misunderstood illustrations in His ministry. In our attempt to make an application of a spiritual principle in a temporal world, we tend to do more harm than good because of our limited point of view. A few points of clarification may help us to understand the truth that Jesus was teaching His disciples.

On the surface, given today's society, it would appear that Jesus is using a totally ludicrous illustration to confirm a widely-held prejudice within the Kingdom of Heaven. When we hear the phrase, our minds envision a twelve-foot tall dromedary being forced through a minute opening at the dull end of a very thin, 1-½ inch piece of aluminum. With the absurdity of such a scenario comes the conclusion of the total impossibility of such an occurrence. Having reached such a conclusion, we then apply it to the object of Jesus' illustration. Consequently, we purport the assumption that there can be no wealthy members in God's family. A quick look at the history of the church demonstrates how errant it would be to hold to such a theory. Certainly, there have been many financially blessed individuals who have very effectively used their wealth to the furtherance of the Kingdom. At that point we find ourselves searching once more for the real truth behind the Master's teaching.

The first thing we need is a little history lesson in the culture, as well as the terminology of Jesus' day. History indicates that the term—"eye-of-the-needle" was applied to a very small gate in the walls that fortified the city of Jerusalem. Though it was passable by the average person, it offered extremely limited access to the common-day beast-of-burden. The society of the day knew that it was not impossible for a camel to enter this gate—as long as it was stripped of all its burdens. Once freed from all its cargo, the animal would then crouch down on all fours, and proceed to inch its way through the small opening. Certainly, it was a long and involved process, but it was not an impossibility.

The most important concept of the illustration is the need to free the animal from its baggage. So it is when a "rich" man comes to the gates of the Kingdom of heaven. Before gaining access, he needs to be relieved of all of the baggage that he has accumulated to that point in his life. Though the articles of luggage may include worldly wealth and the love of money, it may just as likely include such things as life-long dreams and ambitions, social prejudices, bitterness caused by past disappointments or injustices, or any number of similar burdens. It is only after these articles have been taken out of our lives by the healing blood of Jesus, that we can truly "enter in" to the Kingdom of Heaven.

FIRST THINGS FIRST

"But seek first His kingdom and His righteousness, and all these things will be added to you.
Matt 6:33

It began this morning when David Bernard had snapped awake at 6:30am to realize that the alarm that he had set for 6:00am had failed to ring. Upon investigation, he found that, though he had set the time, he had failed to turn the alarm to 'on'. He didn't often use the device—he relied on his 'internal alarm clock' that was permanently set for 6:30am. The flight to Calgary would be available for boarding at 8:00am—that meant that he had to be 'checked-in' by 7:30am. It was time to 'get moving'! There was barely time for a quick shower and shave, a couple of stale muffins and a cup of yesterday's coffee reheated in the microwave oven. Personal devotions were definitely out-the-question this morning—surely the Lord would understand his time constraints.

In his mad scramble to reach the airport on time, David hardly noticed the yellow light about to turn red. There was no other traffic on the street this early in the morning, and, with only twenty feet to go before the intersection, he decided that, in the interest of safety, he would try to 'make it'. He felt a pang of conviction as the car slid under the red traffic light, and he glanced in the rear-view mirror, just to check that there were no red-and—blue flashing lights. His moment of satisfaction was extinguished when he caught the reflection of the flicker from the traffic surveillance camera.

When he finally reached the check-in gate at the airport, he noticed on the screen that his flight had been delayed for thirty minutes while ground crews completed routine maintenance. "Oh great!" he fumed, "now I'll probably miss my flight out of Calgary!" Why wasn't anything going right today? *But seek ye first the kingdom of God . . .* again that small voice penetrated his conscience.

Surprisingly, and much to his relief, the interchange at the Calgary airport went relatively smoothly. The connecting flight had also been delayed for some time—coincidentally, just long enough to accommodate the passengers travelling on to Vancouver. *And we know that all things work together for good to them that love God . . .* The thought was lost as David scrambled to obey the "fasten seatbelts' sign, while the flight attendant explained the features of the aircraft to the disinterested passengers.

An hour later, David sat rigid in his seat as the 737 bounced over the Rockies, dodging a variety of air pockets, making him wish he had left the morning's hurriedly eaten muffin in the refrigerator. The man in the adjacent seat seemed intent on striking up a conversation, but David didn't feel like being talkative right now. After several unsuccessful attempts, the fellow-traveler finally 'got the message' and settled down to read his Financial Post magazine. *Go ye into all the world and preach the Gospel to every creature . . .* Minutes of silence were broken when the voice of the pilot was heard on the intercom, advising the passengers that they would be starting initial descent into Vancouver in five minutes.

The first item on the carousel was a tan-colored suitcase with a green baggage tag—definitely not the one for which David Bernard was waiting. Not that he really expected to be the first in line, but he was in a hurry to catch the shuttle-bus to downtown. He lingered with rising impatience as he realized that the passengers for the shuttle were already congregating outside the terminal door. More luggage was entering the carousel now, and still David waited. Having inspected each item without seeing anything familiar to him, he felt a rising panic as he realized that, for the second time, the burgundy carry-all was the lone item circling on the moving belt. Making his way toward the customer service desk, David noticed that the shuttle bus had departed from it's parking spot.

"May I help you, Sir?" the young man with the starched white-collared shirt asked benevolently. David was irate now, and though it was against everything he had taught his Teen Sunday School class last week, he heard himself bark impatiently at the attendant.

"Where's my luggage?" he growled. "Flight 1107 from Calgary—two blue leather suitcases-they're not on the carousel!"

The customer service representative continued to smile congenially—he had dealt with irate travelers many times. After confirming David's travel itinerary, he made a few short, pertinent telephone calls. "We're sorry Sir, but it seems that one baggage cart was overlooked earlier," he explained, "those item's should be on the carousel within a few minutes."

"Well, thanks a lot!" David complained sarcastically, "now I've missed the shuttle to the Holiday Inn downtown. I am surrounded by a bunch of incompetents!" *In everything, give thanks, for this is the will of God concerning you* . . . but how could anyone be thankful for such a mixed-up day? In the interest of customer-relations, the young man assured David that the airline would provide a voucher for a taxicab to take him to his intended destination. He could tell that this was going to be a long night. He had a few appointments booked for 9:00am tomorrow morning—it was now almost 10:00pm.

When he finally closed the door to his hotel room, it was 11:45pm, and David was livid. It wasn't until he had turned off the bedside lamp that his mind slowed down enough to consider the day. *Good-night David*, he heard that still, small voice whisper to his spirit. Instantly, he was wide-awake, as scenes of the day replayed in his memory like a poorly directed horror movie. He remembered that, in the rush of the early morning, because of the fiasco with the alarm clock, he had failed to spend time in the Word and prayer. "But Lord," he argued, "there just wasn't time!" He remembered his premature frustration at the news of the delayed flight. "Well, at least that wasn't a complete disaster", he comforted himself. He thought of the misplaced baggage cart, and his reaction to the customer service rep. In his spirit, he heard the early morning admonition of the Word—*but seek ye first the kingdom of God, and His righteousness, and all these things shall be added unto you* . . .

"That was the key, wasn't it Lord?" he asked in the silence of the room. "So many of today's disasters could have been avoided by making time for You this morning." Slipping to his knees by the bedside, David humbled himself before Almighty God. After several minutes of prayerful repentance, he felt The Father once again putting His arms around the wandering son. As he drifted off to sleep, he thought he heard a heavenly choir singing . . .

> *Seek ye first the kingdom of God,*
> *and His righteousness,*
> *And all these things shall be added unto you,*
> *'Allelu, 'Allelujah!* . . .

If we can be honest with ourselves before God, we will have to admit that we have all had 'one of those days'. We didn't start with any intention of being rude to the Almighty, but, in retrospect, we are forced to admit that our whole day would have been so much better had we spent the first few moments seeking His kingdom, and His righteousness. It probably didn't take too long, as the day progressed, to begin to notice the consequences of our negligence. What began as a mild irritation, probably escalated to the level of annoyance. Perhaps words of gentle rebuke to family members and friends inevitably turned harsh and defensive. Soon, our thoughts were filled with statements of open rationalization under the conviction of the Holy Spirit.

Still, before we waste an entire day due to our own negligence, it is comforting to know that, at any time, we can redeem the day. It takes only a few moments in the presence of the Almighty to plead forgiveness for any errors or omissions that have been recorded in the heavenly record-book. Having effected such action we will find that God is faithful and just to forgive us our sins, and to cleanse us from all unrighteousness.

THE KINGDOM WITHIN

Neither shall they say, Lo here! or, lo there! for, behold, the kingdom of God is within you.

Luke 17:21

When Jesus taught about the Kingdom of Heaven, the people grew anxious. As they understood the ancient prophecies, the Messiah was coming to set up a political system of peace and righteousness. It would be a place where they would be free from the political tyranny to which they had been exposed repeatedly in their history. The Messiah would physically take His place on the throne of David and rule the nations with justice and equity. For three years they waited for Jesus to *make his move*. Finally, in exasperation the forthrightly asked Him one day—"Lord, when are you going to restore the kingdom?" But it was quite obvious that Jesus was not motivated by political power. His teachings did not embrace the principles of human jurisdiction. Rather, He spent His time teaching about life principles, spiritual ethics, and righteous modes of conduct. It was more important to Him that the disciples learn every aspect of how to experience and propagate the rightful God-ordained authority in every area of their human existence.

And so Jesus taught the multitudes that the rule or authority of God starts as insignificantly as a mustard seed, but grows and develops into an unmistakable part of every believer's life. He made sure that they understood that the influence of the heavenly force would slowly, but surely permeate every facet of their existence. He wanted them to know that in order to fully experience God's purpose for their lives, they would need to disregard everything else that they held dear. The restoration of justice and equity for which they longed would be the result of a diligent search during which they would need to discern the genuine from the counterfeit, and ultimately be prepared to give everything in order to achieve their goal.

My kingdom is not of this world Jesus told the frustrated Roman governor. The statement assures us that the kingdom which the righteous will inherit can only be spiritually appraised. It is not confined to earthly time and values, but must be considered in terms of eternity. Still the principles are as relevant as today's newspaper, and are applicable to any of life's experiences. And so it is my hope that, in the pages of this book you have identified people and circumstances from your own experience, and have been able to see how God's unchangeable principles can be applied to your personal life.

Get Published, Inc!
Thorofare, NJ 08086
23 September 2009
BA2009266